The Coaching Process

A Practical Guide to
Improving Your Effectiveness

To my family, Bob, Matthew and Simon, who provide me with inspiration.
L.K.

The Coaching Process

A Practical Guide to Improving Your Effectiveness

Lynn Kidman
and
Stephanie Hanrahan

Cartoons by
Sharon H. Clough

The Dunmore Press

©1997 Lynn Kidman and Stephanie Hanrahan
©1997 The Dunmore Press Ltd

First Published in 1997
by
The Dunmore Press Ltd
P.O. Box 5115
Palmerston North
New Zealand

Australian Supplier:
Federation Press
P.O. Box 45
Annandale 2038 NSW
Australia
Ph: (02) 9552-2200
Fax: (02) 9552-1681

ISBN 0 86469 285 4

Text:	Baskerville 10/12.5
Printer:	The Dunmore Printing Company Ltd
	Palmerston North
Cover design:	Katherine McGougan
Cover photographs:	Michael Chu, Lynn Kidman, Sportsnews

Copyright. No part of this book may be reproduced without written permission except in the case of brief quotations embodied in critical articles and reviews.

Contents

Preface	7
Section 1: Introduction	11
1. **Successful Coaching**	13
- Coaching Effectiveness	14
- The Enjoyment of Coaching Athletes	16
2. **Developing a Coaching Philosophy**	21
- Fair Play	22
- A Coaching Philosophy	30
- Writing Your Coaching Philosophy	32
Section II: Athlete Development	37
3. **Your Athletes**	39
- Characteristics of Athletes	39
- Athlete-centred Approach	46
- Developing a Team from a Collection of Individuals	49
Section III: The Training Session	55
4. **Developing Managing Skills**	57
- Planning an Effective Training Session	57
- Managing the Environment	69
- Managing Time During Training	73
5. **Creating a Positive Environment**	81
- Positive Approach	82
- Communication	86
- Motivation	92

6.	**Instructional Techniques**	102
	- Demonstrations	103
	- Explanation	106
	- Questioning	110
7.	**Enhancing Skill Technique**	119
	- Observing and Analysing	119
	- Effective Feedback	123
8.	**Enhancing Performance with Mental Skills**	131
	- What are Mental Skills?	131
	- How to Include Mental Skills Training with Physical Training	137
9.	**Coaching During Competitions**	149
	- Developing a Pre-competition Routine	150
	- Developing a Competition Plan	151
	- Self-control	153
	- Extra Jobs when Travelling with a Team	155

Section IV: Factors Influencing Coaching — 159

10.	**Parents**	161
	- A Coach–Parents Meeting	163
	- Communication During the Season	167
	- Expectations of Parents	168
11.	**The Balancing Act**	173
	- Time Management	173
	- Facility and Equipment Management	179

Section V: Continuing to Develop as a Coach — 187

12.	**What Now?**	189
	- Self-reflective Analysis	189
	- Continuing to Develop as a Coach	195
	- Sharing Ideas	196

About the Authors — 199

Index — 201

Preface

The purpose of *The Coaching Process: A Practical Guide to Improving Your Effectiveness* is to enable coaches to provide athletes/players, of all levels, with the best possible sporting experience. The aim in coaching should be to provide a sporting environment where athletes can achieve success. This success can be measured by athletes' satisfaction and improvement.

As coaches, we are always looking for opportunities to identify and practise effective coaching strategies. As we are often left to our own devices, it is difficult to know what to improve, how to improve, or if, indeed, we have improved. Coaching courses are renowned for providing valuable information about sport, but most courses do not provide a way to apply this information to coaching. To provide athletes/players with the best opportunity to strive for success, coaches need to apply more coaching techniques and strategies. In *The Coaching Process* we challenge you, through a self-directed approach, to enhance your coaching. The self-directed approach is an educational tool that enables coaches to apply coaching strategies to their own setting, then encourages them to reflect on how the coaching strategies were applied. *The Coaching Process* is designed so that you can learn at your own pace.

The Coaching Process attempts to acknowledge the complexities of coaching by addressing selected coaching strategies. These are introduced, discussed and evaluated in the chapters of the book. Examples of various coaching strategies and solutions as to how to implement them most effectively are provided.

In each of the chapters, there are activities and/or self-reflective tasks that will enhance your thought process about coaching. Self-reflection provides a non-threatening means of analysing our coaching without the outside pressures of job security or political implications that we can encounter as coaches. Every situation, every athlete and every coach is different. Self-reflection provides us with a tool to determine our effect on those we are working with in sport. Being successful is not measured by how many competitions are won, but by how many athletes continue to happily and successfully participate in sport.

Features of the Chapters

Introductions

Each chapter includes an introduction about the topic covered. It includes information about why the topic was chosen, insight into the experiences of coaches who have applied the particular coaching strategy, and how that strategy is linked to other coaching strategies covered in the book.

Information about a Coaching Strategy

Each chapter provides a base of information under different headings about a coaching strategy. It introduces the theory of the strategy and provides practical examples of the strategy. The practical examples are designed to provide experiences that may relate the theory to a 'personal' situation and bring in situations that occur in 'real life'.

ACTIVITY

The activity sections in each of the chapters provide opportunities to apply information about the coaching strategies to individual sports settings. The activities are written as a 'workbook' approach with tables and short-answer questions provided. These activities encourage further thought about situations that may arise in coaching. **If you choose to write in this text, consider using pencil. You may prefer to use a separate notebook that will serve as a record as you change and monitor strategies and continue developing as a coach.**

SELF-REFLECTION

Recent research has confirmed the value of the appropriate use of self-reflection to enhance coaching strategies. The self-reflection exercises will provide you with a way to practise a selected coaching strategy and you will be able to apply what you have learned to your own coaching situation. You will be able to practise the task without the pressures of 'someone looking over your shoulder'. After attempting the coaching strategy at your own pace, you will be able to analyse and reflect on how the coaching strategy was applied. The learning and changing of these coaching strategies is entirely in your hands. You can experiment and try different methods to apply coaching strategies and therefore find the best method for your own and your athletes' needs.

Using Videotaping in Self-reflection

As part of the self-reflective process, coaches are asked to videotape themselves coaching. Accessing a video camera should be fairly easy; ask friends, family or sport organisations if there is a video camera that can be used. There is always a parent or friend who will 'volunteer' to videotape you while you are coaching. The video will provide you with valuable insights as to how athletes are coached and challenged.

Using Audiotaping

Audiotape analysis is another effective self-reflective aid. Some coaching strategies can be practised using audiotaping instead of videotaping. For example, comments can be recorded to analyse your feedback or questioning skills.

Reflective Questions

To enhance the self-reflective process, reflective questions are included to provide structure and guidelines about specific coaching strategies. We know that effective coaches often analyse themselves to seek better ways to coach. They often ask questions such as, 'Did that work?', 'How did the athletes respond to that approach?', or 'Was that the right way, or should I have tried something different?' We hope that the reflective questions we have provided will facilititate self-analysis to determine what works and what doesn't work.

POINTS TO PONDER
'Points to Ponder' throughout the text can be related to your coaching, someone else's coaching or your athletes. Draw on your own experience to determine a solution where necessary. Sometimes these points may be in the form of quotes from other well known coaches or sports participants.

POINTS TO REMEMBER
Important 'Points to Remember' about coaching will also be given. They may be points for consideration, or essential points that should be applied to coaching.

Summary

Chapters conclude with a summary of points about particular coaching strategies and provide an overall summary of the chapter. A list of readings is provided for those who wish to seek more information on the topic.

Acknowledgements

This book was made possible by athletes, students and coaches who have contributed, discussed, trialled and reflected. These people are the backbone of sport and we thank them for their input. We wish to express our gratitude to Chris Smethurst, Kathy Manu, Ross Sanders and Doug Manu who spent hours reading and providing feedback to drafts of the book.

The Coaching Process

Section I

Introduction

Chapter 1

Successful Coaching

- Coaching Effectiveness
- The Enjoyment of Coaching Athletes

Success is defined in terms of outcome. The *Australian Oxford Dictionary* defines success as 'a favourable outcome; attainment of what was desired or attempted'. In sport, traditionally an outcome is seen as winning or losing a particular competition. This is a very narrow and limited view of outcome.

As coaches we can have a dramatic impact on the development and lives of athletes. What is considered to be successful coaching is dependent on what coaches desire or attempt to achieve.

ACTIVITY

Write down the three main things you want to achieve as a coach. (Remember to use a pencil or photocopy this page to preserve your book.)

1.

2.

3.

> **POINT TO PONDER**
> Think back to a favourite coach. What was it about that coach that you admired so much? What characteristics did he or she have that made you want to learn about that sport? What were that coach's motivating qualities? Have you adopted some of those qualities? Now, think back to the teacher or coach that you disliked. What qualities did he or she have that you would never adopt?

Coaching Effectiveness

Effective coaching is an ongoing process. Coaches do not just complete an instruction course, coach for a specified period of time and then, 'presto', are perfect coaches. Effectiveness is a matter of degree, but there is a persistent belief that we can always improve. As we continue to coach, we constantly refine and enhance our coaching skills. It is important to judge the effectiveness of that process rather than any particular outcome. If coaches are not achieving success (however it is defined), they need to look at changing what they are doing, that is, changing the process. If coaches are successful, they want to be aware of the process so they can maintain their coaching effectiveness.

ACTIVITY

For the behaviours in the following list, mark with an 'S' the points you believe are an indication of success (the outcome you are trying to achieve), or an 'E' aspects of effective coaching (part of the process). Some items may be marked with both 'S' and 'E'.

- ___ Being flexible to meet the individual needs of athletes
- ___ Willing to experiment with new ideas
- ___ Valuing the coach–athlete relationship
- ___ Understanding and appreciating human nature
- ___ Being honest and strong in character
- ___ Being committed to individual integrity, values and personal growth
- ___ Making athletes feel comfortable and happy with training sessions and competitions
- ___ Providing athletes with accurate technical information
- ___ Having fun
- ___ Appreciating individual differences
- ___ Understanding the value of time
- ___ Cherishing the satisfaction of perseverance
- ___ Comprehending the meaning of effort
- ___ Discerning the dignity of humility
- ___ Developing character
- ___ Being kind
- ___ Appreciating the rewards of cooperation
- ___ Valuing/developing friendships
- ___ Learning new skills
- ___ Meeting challenges
- ___ Overcoming obstacles
- ___ Experiencing new things
- ___ Having a positive sense of self (feeling good)
- ___ Feeling it is O.K. to make mistakes
- ___ Winning

___ Communicating effectively
___ Getting recognition
___ Maintaining involvement (being active throughout life)
___ _____

Now go back and look at the responses. Are there common themes in what you have stated is an indication of success and what you have stated is an indication of effective coaching? These concepts will be revisited in the next chapter when your coaching philosophy is developed or refined.

> POINT TO PONDER
> Why do you coach? This may seem like a simple question, but please take some time now to answer.

Self-reflective Learning Process

It is likely that you are reading this book because you are interested in improving your effectiveness as a coach. What you have probably already realised is that developing as a coach is an ongoing process. As mentioned in the preface, you are asked to reflect on current coaching practices. Before determining what changes need to be made, it is important to be aware of how you coach. More than one technique can be used for self-reflection.

One of these techniques is the use of video. Throughout the text coaches are asked to videotape themselves coaching. Many coaches use this technique to enhance their effectiveness. At first coaches may find it a frightening task. Confronting yourself on videotape is daunting, but once past confronting your physical image, looking at coaching strategies becomes easier. After you have become accustomed to your personal mannerisms, you can begin to reflect on your coaching. Videotaping is a useful tool for self-reflective learning in teacher education and has also proven to be effective in changing and monitoring coaching behaviours.

Reflective questions are often a part of the learning process to provide structured guidelines and information about coaching behaviours. Such questions are used to direct coaches to focus on particular aspects of coaching. Reflective questions can be designed by you or any other expert.

Another useful aid in the self-reflective process is a second opinion. By obtaining feedback from another respected colleague, coach or teacher the self-reflective processes in coaching will be enhanced.

Hints for Participating in Self-reflection using a Videotape and Feedback from Others

1. Remember that people generally go through a *self-confrontation phase* when viewing themselves on a videotape (i.e. 'I didn't know that I was so fat', or 'I didn't know that my nose was so big'). Coaches are no different, but the good news is that it passes and attention can then be given to coaching strategies.

2. Ensure the video camera is *focused on you, the coach.* Observing your own body signals is important.
3. Use this book as a guide to the *'how to'* of coaching. Use the reflective questions provided or design questions based on information gathered.
4. Remember that learning a coaching skill is like learning a physical skill. *It takes practice.* When focusing on improving a particular coaching skill, other coaching skills may falter. This is to be expected. Coaching strategies will begin to gel the more they are practised.
5. When searching for someone to provide coaching feedback, pick someone you *respect and trust,* a critical friend.

Self-evaluation Technique

Another technique to improve your coaching effectiveness is to complete self-evaluation forms after coaching (both after training sessions and after competitions). What follows is a simple example of a form that should be completed after a coaching session. Later in the book, coaches will be asked to create their own, more detailed self-evaluation form.

Date: _____   Venue: _____

Strategy/Characteristic	Rating (1 never – 5 all the time)
I listened to my athletes	1 2 3 4 5
I was well prepared for the session	1 2 3 4 5
I was positive	1 2 3 4 5
I gave effective feedback	1 2 3 4 5
I was enthusiastic	1 2 3 4 5
I kept my cool	1 2 3 4 5
I treated my athletes equally	1 2 3 4 5
I provided good learning experiences	1 2 3 4 5
I varied my tone of voice	1 2 3 4 5
I found the session enjoyable	1 2 3 4 5

One thing I did really well this session was _____

One thing I want to remember for next time is _____

The Enjoyment of Coaching Athletes

Coaching demands time, energy, preparation, enthusiasm and patience (just to name a few of the requirements). People coach for different reasons. They may have both extrinsic and intrinsic reasons for coaching. Extrinsic reasons are the external rewards that are available. These are not limited to money or material gains such as free sporting equipment or discounted access to venues. Indeed, only a small percentage of coaches get paid for their efforts. Awards, trophies and other less tangible forms of recognition from others can also be extrinsic reasons for coaching. Intrinsic reasons for coaching are based on the personal sense of satisfaction that can be achieved. Intrinsic motivation involves doing things that make people feel competent or self-determining and can have an impact on the way things happen. For example, a coach may gain satisfaction from team performances and the realisation that what the team worked on together has made them achieve their personal goals.

THE PERSONAL SENSE OF SATISFACTION ACHIEVED THROUGH COACHING USUALLY OUTWEIGHS THE GLORY OF AWARDS AND TROPHIES.

ACTIVITY

Write three examples of things that make you feel competent or self-determining when coaching.

1.

2.

3.

Coaches who are intrinsically motivated to coach, coach for the love and fun of that activity and for personal satisfaction. Obviously, enjoyment is a major component of intrinsic motivation.

The media tend to equate enjoyment in sport with winning. Winning is great! Everyone loves to win, but the day to day aspects of participation in sport and of coaching should be enjoyable. For coaches, satisfaction should be experienced whenever any form of success is achieved or when coaches believe they have been effective. A wide variety of experiences in coaching, not just winning the grand final, can be enjoyable and satisfying. The following are just a few examples of stories coaches have told that express satisfaction and enjoyment.

- David, an athletics coach for a squad of moderate performers, ran gym sessions for his athletes. Rather than sticking with traditional gym activities, David created a circuit of activities that he felt were more specific to athletics. Many of the stations in the circuit he designed, making things up as he went along. After a couple of months, David's athletes were not the only ones attending the gym sessions. Word had travelled and athletes from a number of coaches, including the top-level coach with whom he shared the track, were attending his sessions. The success of his programme hit David the day that he actually had to bar athletes from joining the session, as there wasn't enough room.

- A tennis coach, Chris, experimented by designing a series of lessons with the aim of the student remembering what she'd learned in each lesson. After three lessons, it rained for almost a month causing lessons to be cancelled for four weeks. Prior to the next lesson, a number of coaches told Chris that he'd have to start over with such a large break between the third and fourth lessons. He ignored their advice and stuck with his original plan. Chris expected that the student would remember some of what she had been taught more than a month before. He was amazed when the player performed as if there had been no break in the lessons. The sense of satisfaction experienced caused him to change all his coaching plans to follow the same guidelines as his initial experiment.

- Jan, a BMX coach, had an athlete whose bike was damaged so much that it was not rideable. At the last minute, a substitute bike was found. This bike was not the correct size for the athlete, did not have the proper gear ratios and was virtually little better than not having a bike at all. Although a highly skilled and experienced athlete, Jan's athlete found himself well behind during the competition, but continued to do the best he could at every jump and turn. In the end he didn't win, in fact he had one of his worst outcomes ever. Jan, however, was ecstatic with the athlete's performance. He never once complained or made excuses.

- A child with an intellectual disability came to the rink with her school for ice skating lessons. This child would not walk at school or anywhere else outside the home without firmly gripping on to an adult. As the skating lessons progressed (once a week for four weeks), her classmates were learning to turn, skate backwards and stop (without grabbing onto the wall). One or two children even learned simple spins and jumps. The coach's greatest and warmest memory of coaching that year was when the child with the intellectual disability made it across the rink by herself. Even though she walked more than skated, it was an amazing achievement.

Enjoyment does not have to rely on special isolated incidents. Often the enjoyment is the result of seeing athletes having fun, learning new skills, improving their self-confidence, or helping each other out. Sometimes when caught up in the daily frustrations of last-minute changes to schedules, having to cut or eliminate athletes because of lack of space, or dealing with behaviour problems, we can forget about the enjoyable experiences. Every now and then we should remind ourselves why we are coaching in the first place.

ENJOYMENT CAN BE A RESULT OF SEEING ATHLETES HELP EACH OTHER.

ACTIVITY

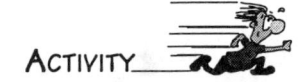

List three things you enjoy most about coaching. These may be specific moments you have experienced.

1.

2.

3.

Summary

1. To become an effective coach, focus on process rather than outcome. Striving to be an effective coach is an ongoing process.
2. Self-reflection is important for improving coaching effectiveness. Techniques facilitating self-reflection include the use of videos, reflective questions and self-awareness forms, and feedback from others.
3. Coaching can be a very rewarding experience, offering both intrinsic (personal satisfaction) and extrinsic (actual or tangible achievements) rewards.
4. The improvement in athletes, the little humorous remarks, the friendships and the memories are just some experiences that make coaching a worthwhile venture.
5. The enjoyment of coaching is an individual experience and is closely related to coaching motivation.

Chapter 2

Developing a Coaching Philosophy

- Fair Play
- A Coaching Philosophy
- Writing Your Coaching Philosophy

THE IMPACT OF COACHES

I have come to a frightening realisation. *I* am the decisive element on the track or on the field. It is *my* personal approach that creates the climate for learning and personal performance. It is *my* daily mood that makes the weather bright or dreary. As a coach, I possess tremendous power to make my athletes' lives miserable or joyous. I can be a tool of torture, or an instrument of inspiration. I can humiliate ... or humor, hurt ... or heal. In all situations, it is my response that decides whether the experience of sport is positive or negative and whether my athletes gain or lose self-esteem.

(Hiam Ginott)

The notion that coaches have as much power as this quotation suggests is astonishing, but real. Power is a word that conjures up many negative images, but by creating and communicating a coaching philosophy, power can be used in a sincere, meaningful way. Coaches have the power to help athletes reach their goals by providing the most positive experience possible. They have the power to increase and maintain integrity in sport because their actions and words have such an impact. Coaches' actions determine the impact of their power because they have the potential to be a definer, creator, provider, deliverer and facilitator of a positive sporting experience. This power is reflected through coaches' personal beliefs, values, principles, and priorities which are the basis for their behaviour. Coaches can influence whether athletes' experiences are full of frustrations or satisfactions, or whether they feel success or failure.

The aim of this chapter is to help develop foundational beliefs about coaching and provide insightful reflection about the coach's role and the importance of developing a coaching philosophy. A coaching philosophy is individual and is based on personal objectives of coaching. The education of athletes is in coaches' hands. For every coach who has educated athletes to have pride, there is another coach who has instilled shame. The coach's role in the education and in the growth and development of athletes is essential to ensuring that athletes are provided with high standards and opportunities to excel. We do not claim that this chapter has all the answers, but it may provide some insight, enabling coaches to reflect on their coaching, seek more knowledge and develop more wisdom.

Fair Play

Ethics has to do with the study of values or moral philosophies and how individuals ought to behave in certain situations. In sport this *correct* behaviour is called sportsmanship or fair play. Coaches acting ethically and in accordance with the principles of fair play will behave as they *ought to,* even in situations where they might want to do otherwise. Self-control is a critical factor. Coaches must develop this self-control, which will help maintain integrity and increase their opportunities of being successful. One of a coach's jobs is to be a mentor for young people. An objective therefore should be to forge in their athletes the strength of character to assure their integrity. Integrity includes honesty, fairness and respect for others. Coaches should be aware of their own belief systems, values, needs and limitations and the effect of these on others. It takes strength of character to maintain integrity; a willingness to stand up for what one thinks is right even when it is unpopular. Integrity is a powerful coaching asset and its absence can drastically affect the tenor of sport for athletes, parents, spectators, officials, supporters and others involved. Integrity is thus not only in one's own interest, as an essential principle to follow for a fulfilling and satisfying life and to gain and maintain self-esteem, but also influences those with whom one works or relates.

Coaches may often be tempted to cheat or take short cuts to impress someone, for monetary gain, or to avoid failure. Each of us probably knows individuals who have succeeded in cheating or taking a shortcut, but the odds are that their behaviour will eventually catch up with them. Cheating can be in the form of trying to fool an individual such as the coach of an opposing team, the opponents, or even an official. The coach, or athletes, or both may be guilty of it. Cheating is unfair not only because of dishonesty, but also because it may result in an outcome that denies another or others a just reward for their efforts. Coaches should remember that condoning cheating or unfair play *is* cheating. Athletes should play or perform their best, but it is the coach's responsibility to keep athletes playing fair when the teams are obviously uneven in skill level.

The concept of fair play thus encompasses not only how an athlete behaves, but also how a coach behaves. Fair play means that coaches and athletes are abiding by the rules, treating the opponent with respect and showing modesty and composure in victory and defeat by not taking unfair advantage of an opposing team or opponent. The concept of fair play is all-encompassing because it can be related to other aspects of

TEACH YOUR ATHLETES TO RESPECT THEIR OPPONENTS.

life. Many believe if athletes learn how to be fair in sport, they will be able to be fair in life. Those who are fair in life, should be fair in sport. Without fair play, any victory becomes hollow and worthless.

A fair-play philosophy in coaching is built on the belief that participation in sport should be a moral pursuit. The fair-play philosophy encourages all to participate in a fair, moral fashion and it extends further – to respect equipment and facilities. The principles of fair play include:

- respecting the rules of the competition
- respecting officials and accepting their decisions
- respecting the opponent
- providing all participants with equal opportunities
- maintaining dignity by setting examples worthy of imitation.

These principles apply to all situations and to all who are involved in sport – coaches, officials, athletes, parents, spectators and supporters.

Rules

The rules and regulations of various sporting endeavours were devised to allow fair competition and fair play. The rules of each sport have generally been thoroughly researched and have continued to be updated as new issues arise. Fair play is based on these rules and whether or not they are followed. Rules give sport its form, its values. Rules are created to enhance the spirit of the game. They are developed by people who care about the sport and have a vested interest in the safety, interests and enjoyment of athletes. Some rules have even been created to enhance the interest for spectators and even now for television viewing. For example, there is a tie-break rule in tennis for television scheduling purposes, and time-outs are taken in basketball for television commercials. Whatever the origin of the rules, coaches have a responsibility to teach and follow the rules of their sport, and to educate young people as to the value of respecting them.

When rugby started in Britain, there was no referee to call the game. The rules were designed by those who played and at that time fair play included a gentlemanly call when a rule was broken. Imagine that concept in today's society. There are already fights between parents on the sidelines, even though there is an official. We now need to get back to the concept of fair play. Rules are created to ensure fair play. Once the coach acknowledges, implicitly or otherwise, that 'rules are made to be broken', the athletes acquire that understanding and the concept of cheating is perpetuated.

> ### POINT TO PONDER
> Children can recite every principle of fair play, but saying and doing are two different things. They have had coaches who value a fair-play philosophy and abide by it through their actions and communication. Those coaches are terrific role models and the children value fair play and act like good sportspeople. However, there have been coaches who say one thing and do another. Children not only talk about the coaches behind their back, but during competitions, they talk back to the referees and the opponents. In some sports, children have been seen spitting in their hands to shake the opponents' hands and the coach on the sideline has laughed, reinforcing behaviour that would likely continue throughout the season.

Officials

The referees, umpires or judges are the most controversial people involved in sport, but are most necessary to keep the competitions fair. Officials do their best, no matter what the spectators and coaches believe. If coaches concentrated more on the game and the notion of fair play, the officials would live a more sedate life. An extreme example of abuse of an official was in a basketball game where a coach was harassing the official. Every time he harassed the official, his team was granted a technical foul. On the third technical foul, the referee threw the coach out of the game. The coach's team was a club team of under-13-year-old girls and the official was 16 years old. His team lost by quite a margin because the actions of the harassing coach influenced the girls so much that they did not have any desire to continue playing. What was the point to this exhibition? What effect would this display have on the players? What effect would this display have on the referee? How many athletes has this coach managed to scare away?

Coaches must come to terms with the purpose of officials in competitions. Both coaches and officials should ensure a fair game by making athletes abide by the rules. Just as coaches have a job to do, officials have a job to do. Just as coaches dislike being criticised and sometimes take the criticism personally, officials feel the same way. Remember that the purpose of officials is also to promote sportsmanship, so coaches should support them. They should shake their hand after the competition and thank them for officiating. It will make their day.

ACTIVITY

Think of three ways of showing officials appreciation and understanding for their officiating at a competition. An example is thanking the officials after a competition.

1.

2.

3.

Opponents

Without opponents, there would be no competition. Respecting the opponents and their abilities is essential to the principles of fair play. Fair play is helping the opponents up when they are injured, or congratulating them at the end of the competition for a job well done. Understanding the abilities and potential of athletes and challenging them to do better demonstrates respect for the opponent, for by trying their best, athletes are giving their opponents an opportunity to demonstrate what *they* can do. If by trying their best, the athletes completely outdo the other team, then coaches have a responsibility to ensure that they do everything in their power to provide the opponents with a more even competition. For example, the athletes' positions could be rotated or athletes given specific goals to work on, such as tactical or skill practice, that do not focus on winning. A golden rule to follow is to treat the opponents the same way you and your athletes want to be treated.

FAIR PLAY?

One of the biggest problems coaches have is the sharing of ideas with other coaches. By sharing information, fair play is enhanced. In other words, by sharing drills, plays and general strategies, the competition becomes more challenging and fair. There are many clubs that are overloaded with extremely talented athletes. Some clubs believe in such an overload, so that they can win all the time. Imagine if we could split the ability levels of the athletes equally among teams. By splitting ability levels, the competition would be enhanced and made fairer. An option for a sport organisation may be for coaches to rate all the athletes and divide the teams into equal abilities. After the team is selected, throw all the coaches' names into a hat and draw teams. Of course, there are advantages and disadvantages to this system. The main advantages would be a fair, equitable starting point for all involved. Some disadvantages could be the logistics of having to travel for training and scheduling training times.

Equity Issues

The United States Olympic Committee (USOC) has written a code of ethics for coaches. The code provides a common set of values so coaches can build their philosophies and provide equitable opportunities for the athletes they coach. Many coaches in the USA are professional, but the general principles of the Code of Ethics should apply to all sports. It is the individual coach's responsibility to advocate a common set of values and to aspire to the highest possible standards of conduct as well as educate his or her athletes to abide by the same high standards.

Coaches should seek to contribute to the welfare of their athletes, which includes considering athletes' individual rights. When conflicts occur, coaches should be able to resolve them responsibly and maturely. If individual rights are ignored, sport will increasingly lose its value as a humanising experience. Just to participate in sport as an individual is joyous. All athletes should be able to experience this joy of participation. Coaches have a legal, ethical and moral duty to ensure all athletes are fairly treated. The equity issues to consider encompass disability, race, gender, ability levels, sexual orientation, cultural considerations, socioeconomic status, and yes, even others which do not appear on this list. Equity is treating everyone fairly and providing everyone with the same opportunities despite differences. Respect the fundamental rights, dignity and worth of all participants. Strive to eliminate biases based on these factors and do not knowingly participate in or condone unfair discriminatory practices. Participants include athletes, families, coaches, officials, volunteers, administrators and spectators. Athletes have a right to an equal opportunity to develop their talents in their chosen sport. They have a right to receive only fair treatment from the coach and their fellow athletes. They need to be encouraged to develop as independent persons who respect themselves and others.

We often have the misconstrued idea that a particular type of person is 'normal'. We think we are 'normal' and we compare our 'normality' to other people. However, there is no normal. Everyone is different in looks, experiences, skill and genetics. Many of us believe if our children do not follow a path we hold to be normal then they are abnormal; but *no one is abnormal* because they follow an alternative path. In sport some have a more difficult time than others, but everyone has something to offer. Not all of our athletes will be Olympic competitors. In fact, very rarely will one ever be an Olympic competitor, therefore Olympic competitors are, by such values, abnormal! Coaches should learn about the athletes who join their team or squad and should provide every possible opportunity for all of them. They should appreciate the team's diversity and provide all members with the best opportunities they can.

Coaches may experience conflict at times, but should accept the obligation to provide an equitable environment for all athletes. You may have to gain understanding of your own biases and why you hold them, and also be aware that messages conveyed, both verbally and nonverbally, are critical to the equitable environment for which you are responsible.

SELF-REFLECTION

All of us have certain biases that may affect our intention to communicate equally with all people. In the list below, write '1' if the word has little influence on your personal biases through increasing numbers to '5' for a word that has great influence.

___ religion	___ culture	___ homosexuality
___ gender	___ body shape	___ dress
___ hair style	___ occupation	___ socioeconomic status
___ behaviour	___ parenting	___ 'élite' athlete

___ physical appearance   ___ type of sport   ___ rival
___ differing opinion   ___ smoker   ___ drug user
___ accessories worn   ___ attitude   ___ drinking problem
___ type of clothing   ___ mannerisms   ___ political activism

By observing the range of your responses, you are acknowledging that the particular biases exist and will then be able to work on reducing them.

Language

Meaning what we say and saying what we mean enhances our values and attendance to equal opportunity. Many equity problems in our society stem from people saying things that contain implicit biases towards a particular person or group. Male gender in language is particularly problematic, yet trying to avoid use of the word 'man' in all words is also problematic. Ensuring that politically correct terms are always used is difficult, but coaches should value the need for the use of correct terminology and strive to achieve it personally. An example is man-to-man defence. Should we say instead, person to person? Does 'son' then signify the male gender? How far do we take the issue? The important consideration here is to ask your athletes which terms they want to use. This, combined with terms that are currently politically correct and include gender, race, disability and cultural considerations, should promote equity. Coaches' best contribution to equality will always be through their own words or actions, to their athletes.

Tips to promote equity:

- Include all sorts of athletes on posters and newsletters.
- Mention all different athletes when discussing sports.
- Do not laugh at or tell racist or ethnic jokes that make fun of an individual.
- Expect that athletes may behave differently.
- Do not allow athletes to tease about equity issues.
- Avoid 'loaded' terms such as bird, queer, sissy, clumsy or wimpy, etc.
- Make sure that low-skilled athletes are not picked last, and assign them tasks they can do successfully.
- Monitor feedback on equity issues.

Are there other strategies that would promote equity in a team?

ACTIVITY

You will need to do this activity with another person – a coach, partner, friend or colleague. Read each case study out loud and discuss the consequences of the case study. What would you do differently? What actions would you suggest?

Case Study One

You are coaching an under-8's soccer team. There are six boys and two girls. This is the first season for both girls and one of the boys, Jason. The other boys have played between one and three years. The girls and Jason are less skilled and do not know the rules of the game. All the boys, including Jason, are always picking on the girls. Even though the coach tends to verbally reprimand the boys, she still laughs when comments are thrown at the girls, like 'you play like girls' and 'what's wrong with you, can't you handle this?' The girls have cried more than once and are ready to quit soccer. Jason is having the time of his life and believes that he has found a great sport to play.

Case Study Two

Kyle (age 10) is an athlete with a hearing impairment, and is quite embarrassed by his disability. When he plays sport, he has to take out his hearing aid and he cannot hear the coach or the other children. Kyle is quite adept at lip reading, but needs to be able to see the person to whom he is listening. When the coach calls all the athletes in, Kyle is often left standing out in the middle of the field, before he realises that he is supposed to be somewhere else. Unless Kyle is close to the coach, he cannot lip read any instructions. The coach does not give Kyle much feedback, because it is so difficult to get him to understand. None of the other athletes have been told that Kyle has a hearing impairment, but some of them are making fun of him and his inability to respond quickly.

Case Study Three

Robert is playing basketball with one of the local high school teams. The coach has called training for Saturdays and unfortunately Saturdays are Sabbath days for Robert and his family. Because of Robert's religious beliefs and commitments, he cannot make Saturday training sessions. The coach has suggested that Robert should not play with his team this year.

Case Study Four

Louisa is an outstanding volleyball player. She has the ability to make the national volleyball team. During her high school team's training session, the coach spends 50 per cent of her time with Louisa. Often the other players are left to fend for themselves. Many of the players are upset about the lack of attention and are beginning to hate Louisa. A couple of the players have approached Ms Bell and complained that they are not getting a fair chance.

Case Study Five

At a Saturday game, your netball team is playing a team from the other side of town. During the game, the coach of the other team continues to verbally abuse her team and puts down players of your team and the referees.

General Guidelines of Fair Play

As a coach you should consider and adopt the following guidelines to ensure a high standard of fair play for teams and/or athletes:

- Emphasise that the process of performance is an important aim in and of itself.
- Ensure your actions are an example of how athletes and spectators should behave; be a good role model.
- Encourage participants to respect the spirit of the game, not just the outcome.
- Actively encourage athletes, parents and spectators to respect officials and other competitors. It should be pointed out that competitors co-operate by competing and that there would be NO COMPETITION without opponents.
- The quality of and participation in the sport experience is more important than who wins or loses.
- Remember that all participants are special and important in their own way and should be treated with respect and dignity.
- Remember that sport is only one aspect of life.
- Listen to what athletes say and adjust your expectations and programmes according to their needs and desires.
- If you are unsure how to handle a situation, talk to another coach confidentially and ensure no names are mentioned.

A Coaching Philosophy

Now that fair play and equity issues have been addressed, we need to begin to formulate our own philosophy based on our beliefs and values. It is a coach's responsibility to communicate a positive philosophy to athletes that will help them achieve their goals. Every sport setting needs guidelines that can be followed and developed. Coaches have the role of defining the nature of these guidelines and following them in the way they coach athletes. By clarifying the guidelines, coaches can make choices and set priorities. For example, if your goal is to develop athletes without considering the outcome of the competitions, this would dictate the coaching methods you would use. Developing a philosophy will enable you to set up the foundations for the entire season and follow through with consistency.

One of the first things to consider is the athletes. Sport belongs to the athletes and coaches should have an athlete-centred approach. A coach's purpose is to develop athletes and increase the quality of sport. The quality of experience that the athletes get out of a season will depend on coaches' value systems, principles and beliefs. If, for example, you decide that winning is the purpose of the season, what will be the implications for the team? What will happen to the less skilled players for instance?

What will you have to give up in order to strive for winning? Are you able to support a philosophy with actions, or are you a 'Do as I say, not as I do, coach'?

> **POINT TO PONDER**
> If we define a winner as someone who tries their hardest to do their best, then we can have a lot more winners.
> (Tom McNab, Athletics Coach)

Success vs Winning

To many, success is measured by how many games or competitions are won or lost. Many coaches' jobs depend on how many matches have been won or lost. Success, however, is not just winning. *Striving to win is more important than actually winning.* An athlete can win without performing well and lose even though the performance has been outstanding.

Winning is important and is a major factor to participating in sports; it allows a comparison with another or others. But success is more important; it is a measure of how well the athletes are participating. Success can be measured by how many athletes come back for more the next year. There are many success stories about famous coaches, but how many coaches have ensured the success of *all* athletes? How many athletes did they scare away because coaches were too adamant about winning? The 'Win at all Costs' attitude is quite prevalent in our society, but there is a heavy cost. In Australia and New Zealand, the first five most frequently given reasons for dropping out of sport are related to the coach.

We do not often hear a coach being described as successful because he or she provided a great environment and encouraged those participating to do their best. The media rarely portrays a successful coach as an educator. However, one of the biggest jobs in coaching is educating athletes – preparing them physically, psychologically and socially. Knowing the athletes and drawing out their full athletic capabilities is success. Coaching is a people job and coaches must know how their athletes tick and what to provide to bring out the best in each athlete. Coaches should have an understanding of and commitment to the individuals with whom they work.

The philosophy of the authors of this book is to provide athletes with caring, trust, positive communication and commitment. This philosophy encourages athletes to be the best that they can be, physically, psychologically and socially. Sport is only part of athletes' lives, not their entire lives, so our measure for success is determined by whether each athlete continues to participate, either with us or with someone else. Athletes have different reasons for participating in sport. Sport offers a breeding ground where athletes gain a sense of competence, achievement and recognition. The important coaches are not only the ones who take athletes to the Olympics or coach an élite professional team, but also the ones who introduce individuals to sport and provide them with self-confidence, success and recognition so that they want to continue with sport. Coaches make the experience positive or negative. Coaches have the power to enable the athlete to succeed. If coaches are dedicated to the pursuit of excellence, that is excellence for the individual, they can offer a profound, enjoyable and positive experience for athletes. Our athletes deserve good coaches, coaches who are dedicated to their betterment and to the development of proud, motivated, successful and happy people.

Writing Your Coaching Philosophy

Chapter 1 has provided an opportunity for you to consider your definitions of an effective coach. It is perhaps an opportune moment to go back and look at the activities completed there and use them to help develop your coaching philosophy. This section will give you the opportunity to write down a personal philosophy. Many coaches have never done this. Most just go and do the job and do not think about why they are there. As mentioned earlier, a coaching philosophy is a personal statement that is based on the values and beliefs that direct your coaching. Try writing these values and beliefs down. Some will feel threatened in doing this, others will be enlightened, but it is important to understand the value systems that guide your coaching and govern your actions. Writing a philosophy clarifies personal values and goals and provides a tangible reference point. You can then constantly check to see that you are abiding by the philosophy. With experience, your philosophy may change and it should therefore be updated periodically.

Children Learn What They Live

Children who live with criticism,
learn to condemn.
Children who live with hostility,
learn to fight.
Children who live with ridicule,
learn to be shy.
Children who live with shame,
learn to feel guilty.
Children who live with tolerance,
learn to be patient.
Children who live with encouragement,
learn confidence.
Children who live with praise,
learn to appreciate.
Children who live with fairness,
learn justice.
Children who live with approval,
learn to like themselves.
Children who live with acceptance and friendship,
learn to find love in the world.

(Anonymous)

Your coaching philosophy will be based on ideas formed from your experiences. Think back to when you were competing, or had a teacher who made an enormous impact. Determine whether those experiences dictate your coaching actions. Your views and opinions may also have been influenced by knowledge gathered over the years. You may have noticed other coaches and said 'I will never be like that because she destroys the athletes. She scared many of the athletes away'. You will also have to look to the future. In what direction do you want the athletes to go?

Coaches are constantly in a predicament as to whether to do what other people say, or to do what they believe. For example, since winning is so important to society and in the media, is it more important to accept the values of the media, or hold on to your own? Do the media need to continue to influence our humanistic approaches by constantly reporting wins and losses?

ACTIVITY

To develop your coaching philosophy, answer the following questions:

1. Why am I a coach?
2. Why are these athletes participating?
3. What do important others think about coaching?

Based on your answers from the above questions, write down the key identified beliefs, values and assumptions of athletes' development, your coaching goals and your views on success. Use your answers to activities in Chapter 1 to help formulate your ideas.

Once the points have been developed, write your complete philosophy. An example of one by Brutus Hamilton (a track and field coach) is provided;

> To create within the athletes an interest and enthusiasm for the events ... then direct that interest and enthusiasm along the lines of sound fundamentals, taught imaginatively, intelligently purposefully and even inspirationally. It sounds rather simple, but it isn't.

Philosophy:

SELF-REFLECTION

After you have written down your coaching philosophy, share it with another coach and discuss the implications therein. Reflect on the following questions:

- How will I communicate my philosophy to my athletes, their parents and administrators?
- How will I ensure I follow my coaching philosophy?
- What happens if my coaching philosophy is challenged? How will I deal with the different values of other people?

Now that a philosophy has been developed and written down, keep it at hand so that you can revise and update it as circumstances change. As you reflect on and challenge your own and others' belief systems, consider the current trends and continue to search for knowledge and wisdom. This book will not have all the answers, but hopefully it will provide ideas for reflection. Question everything you read, and relate it to your own value and belief systems.

Summary

1. A coaching philosophy is based on our foundational beliefs, values, principles, concepts and priorities. A coaching philosophy should govern our actions.
2. Personal philosophies are related to ethics, how people ought to behave in certain situations. Ethical behaviours form the basis of fair play.
3. Having integrity – demonstrating self-control, honesty, fairness and respect for others – is a powerful coaching asset.
4. The principles of fair play include respecting the rules of the competition, respecting officials and accepting their decisions, respecting the opponent, providing all participants with equal opportunities and setting examples worthy of imitation.
5. Coaches have a legal, moral and ethical duty to ensure that the individual rights of athletes are respected.
6. Striving to win is more important than actually winning. Winning allows coaches and athletes to compare themselves to others, whereas success is a measure of how well athletes are participating and athletes compare themselves against themselves.
7. The authors' coaching philosophy is to provide athletes with caring, trust, positive communication and commitment that enables them to be the best that they can be, physically, psychologically and socially.
8. All coaches should take the time to write down their coaching philosophy as the basis for their day to day coaching and their longer-term goals.

Further Reading

Coaching Association of Canada (1988), *Coaching Theory, Level 1: National Coaching Certification Programme,* Gloucester, Ontario: Coaching Association of Canada.

Coaching New Zealand (1993), *Coaches' Fair Play Handbook,* Wellington, NZ: Hillary Commission.

Fuoss, D.E. and Troppman, R.J. (1981), *Effective Coaching: A Psychological Approach,* Canada: John Wiley and Sons.

Launder, A. (1994), 'The Good Sports: A Working Philosophy for Coaches', *Sports Coach,* vol. 17, no. 4, pp. 25–26.

Lumpkin, A., Stoll, S.K. and Beller, J.M. (1994), *Sport Ethics: Applications for Fair Play*, St. Louis, MO: Mosby Year Book.

Martens, R. (1989), *Successful Coaching*, Champaign, IL: Human Kinetics.

Siedentop, D. (1994), *Introduction to Physical Education, Fitness and Sport*, Palo Alto, CA: Mayfield.

Siedentop, D. (1991), *Developing Teaching Skills in Physical Education*, Palo Alto, CA: Mayfield.

Vernacchia, R., McGuire, R. and Cook, D. (1992), *Coaching Mental Excellence*, Dubuque: IA. Brown and Benchmark.

Section II

Athlete Development

Chapter 3

Your Athletes

- Characteristics of Athletes
- Athlete-centred Approach
- Developing a Team from a Collection of Individuals

Being an effective coach is challenging. A coaching approach that works well with one athlete may not work at all with another. Coaches may work hard trying different alternatives and new approaches to teach an athlete a certain skill. Then, after a lot of time and commitment by coach and athlete, success may be achieved. It is a great feeling when finally a way is found to reach a particular individual. However, coaches may feel frustration when the same method does not work with everyone and they have to start the search for another approach.

Yes, coaching is challenging because all athletes are different. These differences, however, make coaching more interesting and ensure we never get bored. The important thing to remember is that all athletes are individuals. How they acquire skills is influenced by their personal differences.

Characteristics of Athletes

Physical Characteristics

Probably the most obvious difference between individuals is their physical appearance. Athletes come in all shapes and sizes. Although body build may contribute to how readily individuals learn particular skills, it is not always necessary to have a particular body build to perform well (or have fun) in a particular sport. For example, being tall can be an asset when playing basketball, but it is not a requirement. A 5'7" (170 cm) player has won the slam dunk competition in the National Basketball Association (NBA) in the United States and a 5'6" (168 cm) player has been a starting member of a professional NBA team. The point is, although a particular body build may be beneficial, it is not a requirement (although there are probably very few jockeys over 6' (183 cm)). As coaches, we should not discourage people, particularly children, from participating in a particular activity just because they do not match an 'ideal' shape. Even though their body build may make it more difficult for them to make it to the élite level (as only a few will), they may get a lot of enjoyment out of participating at a lower level, or may even beat the odds and make it to the top.

Within any group of athletes a range of fitness levels will be represented. Various aspects of fitness will influence how individuals are able to practise physical skills. If Michael, for instance, lacks muscular strength, he will have to put more effort into any activity requiring strength than does someone with better developed muscles. If he has a weakness in part of his body, co-ordination may be affected. Similarly, if Lisa lacks endurance, she may learn a task, but not be able to practise adequately. Seemingly lazy training habits may be due to problems with muscular endurance or aerobic fitness rather than a slack attitude or short attention span. Coaches need to be sure that athletes have the endurance to repeat skills and drills in their sport. Just because some athletes cope well with the work load does not mean that everyone will be able to do the same.

A COACHING APPROACH THAT WORKS WELL WITH SOME ATHLETES MAY NOT WORK AT ALL WITH OTHERS.

Individuals will also differ in their flexibility. Not everyone will have the same range of movement in joints. Poor range of movement in a joint that is important to the development of a particular skill may limit achievement. The issue of flexibility is not just important for sports such as gymnastics or skating where flexibility is an obvious requirement, but for any activity that requires a broad range of movement of a particular joint. For example, shoulder flexibility is needed for correct and efficient technique for backstroke in swimming and for spiking in volleyball. Although Peter may appear to be very fit and co-ordinated, poor shoulder flexibility could limit his achievement as a backstroker or a spiker. Rather than continually repeating drills designed to change his technique, developing a stretching programme to increase his shoulder flexibility would be more beneficial (and probably less frustrating for Peter).

ACTIVITY

Of the athletes you currently coach, write the initials of the athlete you believe to be best and least suited for your sport according to each of the physical characteristics listed. You may have different athletes in mind for each characteristic. Then, in the column provided, indicate what might best help the athlete with the potential disadvantage.

Characteristic	Best	Worst	How to Support or Help
Body Build			
Strength			
Muscular Endurance			
Aerobic Fitness			
Flexibility			

The Senses

Most of us learn about the five basic senses in primary school. We see, hear, smell, taste and touch what is around us. Although athletes' ability to smell and taste have little, if any, bearing on how they learn skills, the other senses play a role in learning most skills. This section will cover the senses of hearing, vision, touch, and also balance and kinaesthetic awareness.

Hearing

The sense of hearing is important. If athletes have a hearing impairment or for some other reason cannot hear clearly, it will be more difficult for them to listen to and understand directions. Even athletes with good hearing may have problems when there is a lot of other noise in the environment or when the person speaking to the group has her or his back to some individuals. Hearing is also important for team sports where calls or suggestions from teammates are common place. Hearing can also provide clues in some sports for how to react to what others are doing. For example, in softball, the sound made when the bat hits the ball can indicate how the ball was hit.

In many sports being able to hear whistles, starting guns or officials is important for athletes to know what they should be doing and when. When coaches or officials are not aware of hearing impairments, they may mistake an individual's inability to hear for a poor attitude or lack of respect.

Vision

Vision contributes to learning and performance in many ways. Probably the most obvious impact of vision in learning physical skills is where athletes are asked to watch demonstrations or models. We often rely on the old saying that 'a picture is worth a thousand words'. Demonstrations can definitely be effective, but for an athlete with visual impairment an equally clear verbal description is needed.

Another influence of vision on learning is so common that it is usually taken for granted by those with good vision. In many activities we get visual feedback about our performance. Whether we are hitting a tennis ball, throwing a javelin or sailing a boat, we learn a lot about the effectiveness of our technique by the visual feedback we are constantly receiving. In coaching situations it is imperative that another way is found for athletes who are blind or visually impaired to receive the same information.

SELF-REFLECTION

Run through a 15–20 minute section of one of the videos of your coaching twice. The first time, turn the sound off and just watch. The second time turn away from the screen and just listen.

- Which sense, hearing or vision, provided you with the most information?
- Are there any sections of the tape that lost meaning when you only watched or only listened?
- If you had an athlete with a hearing impairment, what could you do visually that would make your communication clearer?
- If you had an athlete with a visual impairment, what could you do to more effectively communicate with that athlete?
- What impact would it have on all your athletes if you were equally clear verbally and visually?

Touch or Pressure

The sense of touch is also important when learning some skills. In many ball sports there is an *implicit* acknowledgement that some individuals have better hands, or a better feel, for the ball than others. How you catch a soft sponge ball versus a hard ball is influenced by your sense of touch. How well developed someone's sense of pressure is, can also affect how easily some skills are learned. For example, when swimming freestyle the hand should feel maximum pressure when pushing the water. If you move your hand straight through the water you will be pushing against water that is already moving and will therefore have less pressure on your hand. If, however, you move your hand through a S-shape when pulling it through the water, you will be pushing against still water and therefore feel more pressure on your hand (and move further forward). Understanding the technique intellectually is one thing, but being able to *feel* the difference in the pressure on the hand means the individual once again gets continual important feedback while swimming. If Linda cannot feel the difference in pressure, learning correct technique will take longer because of a lack of feedback. In this situation, patience is needed, as it would be detrimental to Linda for you to mistake her slow learning as a sign that she simply does not understand what she is to do.

Balance

A sense not included in the basic five senses is the sense of equilibrium or body balance. Balance is the basis for voluntary movement and control. Without balance individuals cannot control their movement. An example of this is a newborn giraffe's first attempt at walking. In less than an hour after being born it can stand, but figuring out how to stand and how to walk are two different things. Initially when standing it has all four legs fairly wide apart. When it tries to take a step, it falls in the direction of whichever leg it picked up. The baby giraffe has no control for voluntary movement until it develops a sense of balance. Once that sense of balance is developed, however, the giraffe quickly moves from its hesitant first steps to a carefree frolic.

Sometimes when athletes are having difficulty learning a new skill, it is not because they do not understand what it is they are supposed to do, it is because when trying the skill they are off balance and therefore cannot control their movement. All voluntary movement requires balance if that movement is to be controlled.

> **POINT TO PONDER**
> Consider how balance is necessary for your sport. How might you help your athletes develop their sense of balance?

Kinaesthetic Awareness

Kinaesthetic awareness is being aware of changes in your body position, direction or acceleration. It is related to the sense of touch, but it is more how your body feels when you are moving than how it feels to touch external objects. Athletes with outstanding physical skills have a well developed kinaesthetic awareness. If athletes are not aware of where their bodies are in space or what positions their limbs are moving through, it is very difficult for them to modify technique. How can you change something if you do not know what it is you are currently doing?

Many coaches have probably experienced the situation where they are telling an athlete to move an arm or a leg into a particular position only to have the athlete say that the arm or leg is already there. This is an example of poor kinaesthetic awareness. The person is not trying to be difficult, but honestly believes that the limb is in the correct position. Showing athletes videotapes of themselves can help them develop their self-awareness. It is also useful to continually focus on how the movement feels. Coaches can ask athletes to move through different positions and focus on how the positions feel rather than what they look like.

Personality

In addition to physical or sensory characteristics, athletes also differ in terms of personality characteristics. Aside from the fact that coaches may respond differently to certain personality types more than others, the personalities of individual athletes may influence how they learn skills and cope with competitive situations. There are many personality qualities that could be discussed in this section, but we will limit the discussion to values and attitudes, attentional style, the need to achieve, and anxiety.

Values and Attitudes

Each individual brings with her or him a set of values and attitudes. Although appreciation of individual differences is valuable, it is also important to know that particular values or attitudes may affect learning effectiveness. If Wendy does not value hard work, determination and persistence, it could be difficult for her to fit in with a programme where these values are paramount. If Tony does not respect his coach, chances are that he will not learn effectively from that coach, as anything the coach says will be considered unimportant or incorrect. Athletes' attitudes towards their coaches (as well as the coaches' attitudes towards their athletes) will influence how well athletes learn.

Attentional Style

A person you know could walk past without noticing you because they are so caught up in their own thoughts. On the other hand, some individuals cannot seem to focus on any one thing because they are continually distracted. This relates to their attentional styles. Attentional style refers to how we generally attend to the world around us. There are two dimensions of attention - internal/external and broad/narrow. We may have a tendency toward either an internal focus (our own thoughts or actions) or an external focus (the environment or what other people are doing). Similarly we may tend to have a broad focus of attention (aware of everything that is happening) or a narrow focus of attention (restricting our attention to a particular thought or object).

If Nathan is putting a golf ball, a narrow focus of attention could be useful. However, if Nathan is playing rugby, a narrow focus of attention might result in him turning the ball over to the other team or being flattened by a member of the opposition he did not see. Most sports require our attention to shift at various times. Individuals who are predisposed to a certain attentional focus may find it difficult to change. Coaches may have to create drills to help athletes develop an appropriate focus. For example, in volleyball, the setter should be aware of what the blockers are doing on the other side of the net in addition to focusing on the ball and spikers. Helping athletes broaden their focus of attention could involve getting them used to looking at the other side of the net by holding up coloured paper for them and having them call out the colour before setting the ball. Once they are used to looking at the other side of the net, there could be progressions of the drill that require decisions about setting determined by what is happening on the other side of the net.

ACTIVITY

Determine when in your sport it would be appropriate to have each focus of attention.

Broad and internal:
Broad and external:
Narrow and internal:
Narrow and external:

Now pick one of the above and explain how you could help an athlete develop that focus of attention.

Need to Achieve

Achievement motivation theory suggests that there are two primary motives - the motive to approach success and the motive to avoid failure. People with a strong motive to avoid failure tend to avoid voluntary participation in sport. They would rather not participate at all than take the chance of failing. We all have a bit of both motives. If our desire to approach success outweighs our desire to avoid failure, we tend to choose activities where there is approximately a 50:50 chance of success. We want to have some chance at success, but we also want the success to mean something when we achieve it. On the other hand, if our motive to avoid failure is stronger than our motive to approach success, we will tend to either not participate, or choose options where success is practically guaranteed or virtually impossible. We will pick either the easiest or the most difficult option.

Sometimes when athletes continually clown around and try the impossible, they are hiding a strong motive to avoid failure. If they fail at something at which no one would be expected to succeed, they have not really failed. These individuals need to learn that never making a mistake means never improving. Mistakes need to be looked at in a positive light. If Trish is learning to ice skate and is very afraid of falling, she will probably never let go of the boards. If she never falls, she is never trying something she cannot already do. If she tries something new and falls, she needs to consider what she could do differently to stay on her feet. Learning does not occur when chances are never taken.

Anxiety

Anxiety is the tendency to perceive a situation as threatening, stressful or challenging. An identical situation can be interpreted differently by different people. John may enter a major competition and feel very anxious because he perceives the situation to be threatening. He worries about how he might blow it or let down his coach. Terry might enter the same competition and even with the same level of skill feel that the situation is a challenge. She may feel that she now has a chance to show her stuff.

The tendency to view situations as threatening or challenging relates to individuals' trait anxiety levels, or how they generally perceive situations. State anxiety, on the other hand, relates to how anxious an individual is in a specific situation at a specific point in time. Anything that increases athletes' uncertainty or the importance of the outcome will increase state anxiety levels. When coaches talk about how, 'we've trained all year for this moment', they usually succeed in increasing the anxiety of their athletes rather than making them excited. The more certain athletes can be about their own ability, their position on the team and whether they are liked by their team-mates and coach, the less likely they are to be anxious.

Different Backgrounds

All athletes come to a team with different backgrounds and experiences. Those different backgrounds and experiences will influence how they react to their coach and how they learn. For example, if Sally and Jay are both learning to swim, but one of them had a frightening experience in water when younger, each will approach the water differently. Also, previous coaches will influence athletes' attitudes towards their present or future coaches. Individuals who have had a coach who yelled whenever anyone made a mistake, may be hesitant to try something new. If they had a coach who encouraged feedback, they may offer suggestions even when they have not been asked for them.

A discussion about how backgrounds and experiences influence athletes could take up the remainder of this book. Family and cultural expectations and values, the sporting successes and failures of siblings and parents and societal expectations in terms of gender-appropriate activities are just a few examples of the factors that may influence each athlete. The main thing to remember is that each athlete is an individual and that rather than expecting all athletes to conform, to be clone-like, coaches should be flexible and accommodating of their differences.

Athlete-centred Approach

Athletes participate in sport for many reasons and coaches have to consider their individual motives for being involved in a particular sport. Not only have athletes started the sport for various reasons, but they also have different incentives to continue participating. Coaches should determine what it is that encourages each athlete to participate and continue in sport. Athletes have an incentive to continue when their experience is enjoyable and satisfying. If their experience has not been enjoyable, they will eventually drop out and find a different sport or activity that is more satisfying.

An athlete's motives to participate include affiliation, mastery, desire for sensation, self-direction and social comparison.

Affiliation

An athlete's affiliation incentive is based on a desire to have positive, friendly relationships with others. Athletes with an affiliation incentive are socially reassured by making new friends or maintaining friendships. Coaches should aim to provide an environment that is conducive to social affiliation – make interaction with others a part of each training session. Examples are developing partner drills, encouraging partner stretching, or having participants coach each other. Coaches may also consider having team talks after each training. These should be informal and encourage athletes to be open and honest. It would be useful to encourage athletes to help one another and to do things together. Athletes should be reminded that everyone is a valued member of the team. The provision of opportunities for social get-togethers after competitions can contribute to feelings of affiliation.

Mastery

Another incentive to participate is a desire for mastery. Athletes with this incentive wish to improve skills, master new skills and pursue excellence. If athletes tend to have a mastery incentive to participate, coaches should endeavour to point out individual improvement, keep written records of progress in diaries and logs, arrange regular meetings to discuss progress and re-evaluate athletes' goals. Athletes with an incentive for mastery typically do something well for its own sake. For example, Jimmy has been practising a smash shot in badminton. He is so keen to master this smash shot that he spends a lot of time just improving that shot. When he gets to a competition, he decides to try it on an opponent that he has not been able to beat for a long time. Mastery incentive for Jimmy would be making a great smash shot, but not necessarily beating his opponent.

Desire for Sensation

Another incentive to participate is a desire for sensation. This may be derived from the sights, sounds, excitement and physical feelings surrounding a sport. This incentive focuses on the thrill, tension, pressure and pure action that sport can provide. For athletes who have a desire for sensation, coaches should try to arrange workouts in areas with pleasant sights, sounds, smells and physical feelings. For example, athletes could warm up to music. Coaches should provide enough activity for everyone - not too much, not too little. Within the training session, drills and activities should be provided that are fun and use different resources. Workouts should be varied by changing routines and allowing participants to work on exciting new moves or create new drills.

Desire for Self-direction

Some athletes may also participate because of a desire for self-direction. These athletes have a wish to feel a sense of control or to feel in charge. They should be given responsibilities, for example a position of leadership. Coaches may consider having the self-directed athlete lead warm-ups, or choose drills to develop certain skills. They should give athletes chances during practices or competitions to make their own decisions about what strategy to use (what pitch to throw, what play to run). Above all, coaches should let athletes make decisions when it really matters. This approach helps athletes learn to enjoy the competition and is a valuable learning experience.

Social Comparison

Some athletes participate in sport for social comparisons. They are concerned with comparing themselves to others. Athletes with this incentive seek status and prestige through winning competitions or beating others. They are most happy when they are better than others. A major consideration with athletes motivated this way is that if their skill level is relatively low, they tend to drop out of sport. To cater for these athletes, coaches should include competitive games within the training session, such as relays or games that have a winner and a loser. The purpose of these games is to give points or some other reward to ensure there is an outcome to the various drills that the athletes are practising.

Coaches should remember that athletes can be motivated by more than one of the incentives listed above and differences in athletes' characteristics need to be kept in mind. It is quite possible for coaches to ensure that each athlete has the opportunity to master her or his chosen sport, be given feedback on personal performance, yet at the same time have the opportunity for social interactions. It is important to understand these motivations so that coaches can cater for a variety of needs and athletes are motivated to continue to be involved in the sport.

ACTIVITY

Write the initials of each of your athletes in the table below. Work out the incentive(s) for each athlete's participation motive. In the last column, identify activities or ways that you can ensure the athlete meets his or her motives.

Athlete's Initials	Affiliation	Mastery	Sensation	Self-Direction	Social Comp	Methods to Ensure Athletes Have an Incentive to Participate

Developing a Team from a Collection of Individuals

So far this chapter has focused on how different individual athletes are from each other. While still appreciating individual differences, we usually find that coaching situations are enhanced by having the athletes form a team. Bringing a group of athletes together, however, does not automatically create a harmonious team. Even though athletes may wear the same uniform, rarely do they spontaneously form a cohesive team.

A cohesive team is one where the members like each other and stick together in pursuit of the group's goals or objectives. As with coaching and learning, cohesion is a process. Cohesion does not just happen and then remain as a permanent feature of the team. How athletes feel about each other and work together changes over time. Throughout a team's existence, there is a continual build up and decline of cohesiveness.

There are two types of cohesion: social and task. Social cohesion refers to how much the team members like each other and enjoy each other's company. Even individual sports, where there is no interaction between athletes during competition or training, can benefit from social cohesion. Task cohesion refers to how well the members work together towards achieving the goals of the team. Most interactive team sports such as hockey, soccer or basketball require high levels of task cohesion if the team is to perform effectively. Task cohesion, however, is not limited to interactive team sports. Athletes in individual sports, such as golf or skateboarding, can profit from task cohesion when individuals support each other by giving advice on technique or tactics.

Benefits of Cohesion

Individuals are more likely to remain with the team when it is cohesive. Cohesiveness enhances stability. Although there are examples of élite teams with poor cohesion performing well, cohesiveness generally enhances performance, particularly for interactive sport teams. From an individual point of view, athletes gain satisfaction from being in a cohesive team. Most people prefer teams where there is harmony and unity rather than antagonism and disquiet. In addition, satisfaction is gained from success. When cohesion enhances performance, it also, indirectly, creates satisfaction.

Getting to Know Each Other

When a group of people first come together, they can feel awkward or inhibited because they do not know each other and do not know what to expect. This lack of familiarity can cause hesitant performance in sport. A multitude of ice-breaking activities exist that allow people to get to know each other. A number of them focus on learning names, but ice breakers are usually more effective if they allow individuals to learn more about each other than just their names.

One activity (it can work with both male and female athletes of all ages and ability levels) involves bringing a collection of soft toys and objects to the group. Be sure to have more items than there are people in the group. Display the toys and objects so that everyone can see them, then ask each individual to choose the item that best represents them. It is useful to provide examples such as, 'One of you may think you are like a knife - always getting into everything, fairly sharp and rather direct and to the point. Another may be more like a possum – appearing to be very shy, particularly in new surroundings, tending to fall asleep during the day but being the life of the party after dark'. Do not include in the display the items that you use as examples.

After each individual has selected an object, organise the athletes into pairs where they are to explain to their partner why the item they selected is representative of them. Next, the athletes form a circle and place their objects in the middle of that circle. Then each athlete selects the object that represents their partner and explains to the entire group whom the item represents and why it is an appropriate choice. The activity becomes a fun and creative method of getting to know each other. Sometimes the objects selected in this activity contribute to nicknames that can stick for the season or even longer.

Your confidence in the value of the exercise will influence how much energy individuals invest in the activity. A note of caution: when working with children, make it very clear at the outset that toys and objects must be returned at the end of the exercise. Otherwise you may find a few of the cuddly friends have been kidnapped!

ACTIVITY

There are other ice-breaking activities that you may have used or experienced. Talk to another coach and swap ice-breaking activities. Try to gather three new activities to use with your squad or team.

1.

2.

3.

Trust

One component of cohesion is trust. In a cohesive team, the individual members trust each other. In addition, the development of trust can enhance cohesion. When individuals trust each other, they will be open with their feelings, ideas and information. This openness will enhance communication. Although specific trust exercises and games can be incorporated into training sessions, the day to day behaviour of group members has a powerful impact on the establishment of trust. Individual athletes and coaches can facilitate the development of trust by displaying particular behaviours.

ACTIVITY

For each of the behaviours in the following list, note whether you believe it enhances trust and/or enhances cohesion. (Mark them 'T' and/or 'C'.)

___ Smiling
___ Spending time small-talking about pleasant things
___ Looking others in the eye
___ Having a good laugh with others
___ Listening to others
___ Telling others when you agree with them
___ Shaking hands
___ Confirming that you understand what others have said
___ Including others in your activities
___ Clarifying to make sure you understand others
___ Encouraging others by recognising them for something they have done
___ Finding interests you have in common with others
___ Finding experiences you have in common with others
___ Offering to help others
___ Telling jokes
___ Taking a little risk
___ Feeling free to disagree with others and giving them the freedom to disagree with you
___ Asking others for feedback
___ Co-operating with others
___ Not always disagreeing with others
___ If you do disagree, criticising others' ideas, not them
___ Telling others things that check out
___ Going the extra mile
___ Reassuring others when things aren't going well
___ Sympathising with others
___ Offering constructive criticism
___ Empathising; taking the time to feel how others feel
___ Getting to know others
___ Accepting others for who they are
___ Helping settle conflicts
___ Telling others they are valuable to the team
___ Being honest with others
___ Sharing with others
___ Being sincere
___ Keeping your word
___ Spending time with others
___ Being genuine
___ Saying hello
___ Asking others how it's going
___ Forgiving mistakes
___ (other) _____
___ _____

Now go back through the behaviours that you noted as enhancing trust and/or cohesion. Select three behaviours that you will ask both yourself and your athletes to display during the next few training sessions or competitions. Pick behaviours that you think will have a positive impact on your team. A variation is to present your athletes with a list of behaviours and have them choose the three they want to incorporate.

1.

2.

3.

Developing Cohesion through Creating Distinctiveness

Encouraging team identity by making members of the team distinctive from other teams enhances unity. The most common source of distinctiveness is the team uniform. Other possibilities include everyone styling their hair the same way, applying the same colour of zinc cream, wearing the same bathing cap, or even something as subtle as having team shoe-laces.

CREATING DISTINCTIVENESS TO DEVELOP TEAM COHESION.

Developing Cohesion through Establishing Team Goals

Chapter 5 will go into detail about the process of setting goals. In terms of increasing cohesion, it can be useful for coaches to encourage the group to set team goals and then take pride in their accomplishment. Team goals can provide the individuals of the team with a common sense of direction and purpose. Once two or three team goals have been established, posting the goals at the training venue can serve as reminders about what the team is trying to achieve.

Developing Cohesion through Cultivating Ownership

Athletes need to feel that the team is their team and not the exclusive property of the coach, the school or the club. Ownership is accomplished by allowing and encouraging members to become involved in decisions that affect the team and them personally, such as involving them in decisions about training times, drills or tactics.

ACTIVITY

Select three decisions that you will encourage your athletes to make during the next training sessions that will affect the team as a whole. Determine the process that you will recommend your athletes use to make each decision. For example, will you leave it entirely in their hands, take a vote, or let different subgroups make different decisions?

Decision	Process
1.	
2.	
3.	

Developing Cohesion through Determining Role Identities

All members of a team need to learn their respective roles in that team and come to believe those roles to be important. Each member of a team has a unique role. If individuals do not feel they have something to contribute to the team, then they will not feel they are a part of the team, which in turn will detract from team cohesion. Additionally, each member of the team should be acquainted with the responsibilities of other members and appreciate their importance. In team sports, this appreciation of team mates can be accomplished by either rotating positions during training or performing team drills with one position removed. Playing other positions can help athletes understand the demands on their team mates, and playing without a position highlights the importance of that position.

Developing Cohesion through Avoiding Turnover and Cliques

Ongoing changes in team membership make it difficult for members to establish good rapport. Excessive turnover causes individuals to be unfamiliar with each other and uncertain about the team's durability and permanence. Therefore, to the extent that it is compatible with team requirements, excessive turnover should be avoided. When new members join an existing team, steps should be taken to integrate the newcomers both socially and in terms of task-related roles. Within existing teams, care should be taken to avoid the development of cliques. A clique is an exclusive subgroup of individuals that actively excludes others from joining. Cliques work in opposition to team goals. In fact, studies in basketball and soccer have demonstrated that athletes who like each other tend to pass the ball more often to each other than to less-liked team mates, even when these latter athletes may be in preferable positions. Changing partners during drills, including the integration of newcomers as part of team-meeting agendas, and emphasising activities that require group co-operation will all help develop team cohesion.

Summary

1. Athletes are individuals. How they acquire skills is influenced by their personal differences.
2. Athletes differ in terms of the physical characteristics of body build, strength, muscular endurance, aerobic fitness and flexibility.
3. Athletes' senses of hearing, vision, touch or pressure, balance and kinesthetic awareness influence their acquisition of skills.
4. Personality attributes such as values and attitudes, attentional style, the need to achieve and anxiety influence how individuals behave.
5. The various experiences that individuals have had both in and out of sport will influence each athlete personally.
6. Athletes usually participate in sport for one or more of the following reasons: the need for affiliation, the desire for mastery, the desire for sensation, the desire for self-direction and the desire to gain status and prestige by beating others.
7. There are two types of team cohesion. Social cohesion refers to how much the team members like each other and enjoy each other's company. Task cohesion refers to how well the members work together towards achieving the goals of the team.
8. Cohesiveness can increase performance and satisfaction as well as increase the likelihood that athletes will remain in the team.
9. Trust is a component of cohesion.
10. Cohesion can be developed by creating distinctiveness, establishing team goals, cultivating ownership, determining role identities and avoiding member turnover and cliques.

Further Reading

Canadian Coaching Association of Canada (1988), *Coaching Theory: Level 1: National Coaching Certification Programme*, Gloucester, Ontario: Coaching Association of Canada.

Carron, A.V. (1980), *Social Psychology of Sport*, Victoria, Australia: Mouvement.

Eunson, B. (1994), *Communicating for Team Building*, Brisbane, Qld: John Wiley and Sons.

Sleigh, J. (1990), *Making Learning Fun*, Wollongong, NSW: John Sleigh Management Training.

Straub, W.F. (1978), *Sport Psychology: An Analysis of Athlete Behavior*, Victoria, Australia: Mouvement.

Williams, J.M. (1993), *Applied Sport Psychology: Personal Growth to Peak Performance*, Mountain View, CA: Mayfield.

Section III

The Training Session

Chapter 4

Developing Managing Skills

- Planning an Effective Training Session
- Managing the Environment
- Managing Time During Training

In the first chapter we introduced characteristics and qualities of a successful coach. Planning to maximise learning is one of those essential qualities. Providing an environment that is conducive to learning requires some creative, yet logical, steps. To help coaches develop athletes and ensure a smooth flow to the training session, this chapter will discuss two coaching strategies that create a positive, caring environment: *session planning* and *positive management*. The goal of this chapter is to provide coaches with consistent methods to optimise opportunities for athletes to learn about their chosen sport and about life.

In coach education courses coaches often ask, 'How do I organise these athletes?' 'How do I control these children?'. This chapter provides some guidelines and perhaps some answers to these sorts of questions. We do not suggest that the answers are the only ones; we only want to provide some opportunities for you to learn by thinking about the methods that work best for you when coaching. To continue the pursuit of coaching effectiveness and the best methods of coaching, coaches should continually ask themselves questions like 'Why did this work?', 'Did I achieve my objectives for the training session today?' or 'How can I improve the managing of my athletes in the training session?'.

Planning an Effective Training Session

A good training programme begins with good planning. Many coaches hate to plan, yet planning for the season and each training session is one of the most important aspects of coaching. Failure to plan can lead to disastrous training sessions. Without planning, coaches can spend too much time organising and deciding what to do during the training session. Coaches tend to meet with their athletes for a limited amount of time each week. This valuable time needs to be used for preparing athletes to improve skills and for competitions. If you spend a lot of time organising during training sessions, the athletes have less time to participate in the activities they so love.

One of the important coaching strategies is to be able to provide a variety of learning experiences throughout the season that give athletes a solid foundation from which to improve skills. Coaches need to be aware of unbalanced programmes in which athletes only learn one aspect of the sport. Athletes need to be given opportunities to understand everything about the sport, be able to play every position, or try every event. Most athletes do not stay with the same coach in all their years of participation, so a balanced programme enables athletes to move forward and continue to improve.

It can be very tempting to avoid planning, yet it is an essential aspect of effective coaching. Can you think back to the number of times that you had a teacher or coach who was not prepared? Was there a purpose to each training session? How did you feel about not being able to touch the ball more than once during a training session or only getting one attempt on the vault? Did you understand what you were supposed to do? Did you spend a lot of time moving from one activity or standing in line waiting your turn? These are the sorts of planning considerations that will be addressed in this chapter.

PLANNING.

Designing an Effective Training Plan

Through your education in coaching, you have probably been involved with the process of planning a pre-season, season or individual training session. For the purpose of enhancing individual training session planning and to prepare for future sessions, we ask you later in the chapter to design a training session within your own current season, using a standard format. But first, we will discuss the process of planning a training session.

A first step in the process of planning is to determine your instructional objectives for the training session. By establishing objectives, a coach can select, design and evaluate the learning activities for that session. An instructional objective is a statement describing a *task,* the *situations* under which it will be performed, and the *criteria* or standards by which it will be judged.

There are three domains of learning which should be considered when designing instructional objectives:

1. performance (movement skills)
2. cognitive (knowledge and awareness), and
3. affective (values, feelings, attitudes and emotions).

Performance objectives are those movement skills athletes will perform during the training session. *Cognitive* objectives are the tactics, strategies, rules or other knowledge-type learning that athletes are to gain during the training session. *Affective* objectives are the attitudes and values expected in the training sessions. Coaches are generally most concerned with the performance objectives, but all three domains should be encompassed and planned in each training session. When developing objectives remember that they should be achievable. Objectives should be written as outcomes that can be measured and evaluated. You should attempt to incorporate all three learning domains in every training session to enhance the holistic learning of the athlete.

To help develop your session objectives, here is a sample format of a basketball session:

Performance objective:
The athletes will be able to perform all aspects of the lay-up (task), starting from the half court line (situation), and be able to make nine out of 10 lay-ups with the dominant hand (criteria).

Lay up	From half court	9 from 10-dominant hand
Task	**Situation**	**Criteria**

Cognitive objective:
After two fitness sprints, athletes will locate and count the pulse for a 10-second interval.

Locate and count pulse	After fitness sprints	For a 10 second interval
Task	**Situation**	**Criteria**

Affective objective:
Athletes will demonstrate co-operation by listening quietly when the coach gives directions.

Listening	During directions	Without talking
Task	**Situation**	**Criteria**

ACTIVITY

Write down objectives for the next training session that you will coach. Remember that you may have more than one objective in each domain of learning.

Performance objective:
_____
_____

Task	**Situation**	**Criteria**

Cognitive objective:
_____
_____

Task	**Situation**	**Criteria**

Affective objective:
_____
_____

Task	**Situation**	**Criteria**

Now that you have established the objectives for a training session, ask yourself, 'What will the athletes need to do to achieve each instructional objective?' The answer will contain a list of skills, knowledge and behaviours (tasks) that athletes will need to achieve the objectives. By developing this information the content of the training session will be structured. To develop the content of the objectives listed in our examples, we need to consider the main skills, knowledge and behaviours (tasks) first.

Examples:

Performance objective: *The athletes will be able to perform all aspects of the lay-up (task), starting from the half court line (situation), and be able to make nine out of 10 lay-ups with the dominant hand (criteria).* The main task needed to ensure this objective is met is lay-ups.

Cognitive objective: *After two fitness sprints, athletes will locate and count the pulse for a 10-second interval.* The main tasks needed to ensure this objective is met are running and taking their pulse.

Affective objective: *Athletes will demonstrate co-operation by listening quietly when the coach gives directions.* The main task needed to ensure this objective is met is listening.

ACTIVITY

Using the above as an example, list the main skills, knowledge and/or behaviours (tasks) for the objectives you wrote in the previous activity.

Your performance objective tasks needed:

_____

_____

Your cognitive objective tasks needed:

_____

_____

Your affective objective tasks needed:

_____

_____

After establishing the tasks, you have to decide on the instructional process to be used. The instructional process is developed by working backwards from each task you listed above and determining which parts of each task are essential to learn so the final objective can be met. After breaking down each task, you will need to establish every *sub-task* the athlete should know and/or perform. A sub-task is a part of the task that is required to perform the terminal task. These sub-tasks form a chain of events that produce the task required. By identifying these sub-tasks, you can decide on the instructional process to teach the skill, knowledge or behaviour. This instructional process is called a *task analysis* (also used in Chapter 7).

Performance example objective:
> To do a lay-up, the athlete should be able to first perform:
>> the dribble
>> the run-up
>> the take off
>> a shot
>> the landing

Cognitive example objective:
> To take her pulse after some fitness work, the athlete should be able to:
>> run
>> locate a pulse
>> count the pulse
>> multiply by six

Affective example objective:
> To demonstrate co-operation by listening quietly, the athlete should be able to:
>> show eye contact
>> raise his hand when waiting to speak
>> follow what you are saying

ACTIVITY

List the sub-tasks that are needed to perform the terminal tasks from the objectives you have set:

Your performance objective:

_____   _____   _____
_____   _____   _____
_____   _____   _____

Your cognitive objective:

_____   _____   _____
_____   _____   _____
_____   _____   _____

Your affective objective:

_____   _____   _____
_____   _____   _____
_____   _____   _____

Once you have completed the task analysis for each of the objectives of the session, it is important to develop coaching cues. Coaching cues are words that serve as reminders to the athletes about how to perform the task. For example, a cue for completing a lay-up would be 'follow through'. It is also useful when learning new skills for the athletes to have cue words or phrases that serve as a visual image for the skill. For example, in rowing the completion of a rowing stroke could be 'think of a spring to accelerate and decelerate the rowing stroke'. Cues also provide convenient reminders so the athletes can practise the skills on their own, or outside of training sessions. Another example of cues that we may use for a spike in volleyball might be 'wrist snap' or 'high elbows'.

Summary of Task Analysis

The following is from a session on basketball using the performance objective from the lay-up example and should summarise what has been covered thus far:

(a) Instructional objective:
    The athletes will be able to perform all aspects of the lay-up (task), starting from the half court line (situation), and be able to make nine out of 10 lay-ups with the dominant hand (criteria).
(b) Content:
    lay-up
(c) Task analysis:
    dribble
    run-up
    take off
    shot
    landing
(d) Cue words:
    Dribble: push the ball in front
               keep the ball below your belly button
               eyes up
               use your finger pads
               protect the ball
    Run-up: dribble
    Take off: like a hurdle in diving
               lift your knees and arms
               a puppet on a string
               same leg as shooting arm
               lift up

Shot: flexed wrists
          follow through
          aim for an upper corner
          push it up
Landing: bend knees
          balance and run through

ACTIVITY

Identify and list cue words or phrases that you might use for the content you have selected for your training session.

Cue words or phrases for your task analysis content:

_____
_____
_____
_____
_____
_____
_____
_____

After identifying the cue words or phrases, analyse what you have written by answering the following questions:

- Are the cues relevant to the execution of the task?
- Do you use visual imagery to provide realistic comparisons?

The Training Session Plan

Thus far, you have (a) developed objectives for your session (b) identified the content (c) completed a task analysis and identified the sub-tasks, and (d) listed cue words for the tasks. You now need to design the learning activities that will meet the requirements of the selected content. After selecting the content, you will need to choose the teaching methods that will be used. When finalising the plans about how to teach the tasks of the training session, it is important for you to think about the process of learning the task. The sizes of the steps that are taken from one sub-task to the next are important because if the steps are too large, athletes can experience failure and lose the motivation or enthusiasm necessary to perform the task successfully. If the steps are too small, the athletes can become bored. Try to establish steps that are large enough to continually challenge the athletes and small enough so that they can experience frequent success.

Point to Remember
A coach's plan is only as good as the coach's execution and management of the plan. Be flexible. Coaching is extremely complex and you need to be ready for the unpredictable.

Planning for Different Ability Levels

One of the many challenges coaches have is to provide all athletes with maximum opportunity to improve and practise their skills. All levels of the athletes' skill abilities must be considered. Coaches may have a tendancy to give more time to the higher skilled athletes because they want to ensure that their athletes reach their highest ability, or they may tend to focus on the lower skilled athletes because they need the most help. By focusing on one skill level, other athletes tend to be ignored. Consider some of the games and drills that are played, like touch rugby. In touch rugby, if a lower skilled player is put as a wing, the player's rate of success may be decreased because the player will hardly ever get to touch the ball. In a novice game of touch rugby, invariably the action is in the middle of the field and therefore any player on the wing probably has little contact with the ball. Elimination games tend to inhibit athletes' rates of success. The lower skilled person is almost always the first to get eliminated, thus taking away the opportunities to practise for success. For example, in basketball, when an elimination game is played (where each player tries to get the ball into the basket before the player in front of her), the player that gets knocked out first, is usually the one that does not shoot as well as the others. Therefore, the low-skilled athletes' success rate in such a game is minimal.

The Grid System

Coaches often plan training sessions where there is only one entry level to a skill. Coaches need to provide quality learning experiences where all get a chance to practise at their own skill level. An example of a successful method to organise athletes and ensure all can practise at their own skill levels is the *grid system*. The grid system is a teaching approach to increase the number of opportunities for athletes to practise. The grid system is an organisational strategy where grids are formed and athletes practise within the grids. The advantage of using grids is that large groups can be organised efficiently. A grid is a marked off playing space area (see Figure 4.1). The marked grid can be any size that is required to complete a drill.

The grid system is an individualised learning approach that allows relatively easy monitoring of athlete skill acquisition. A coach can observe performances effectively, correct individual faults and acknowledge proper execution of skill. A coach can observe from the outside of the grid or observe as he or she walks through. Remember that for safety, you should never have your back to any athlete. Figure 4.1 provides a sample of a grid. The lines are boundaries and each corner of the grid should be marked with a cone or other marker.

A grid coaching area can be utilised for a number of different drills:

- All athletes practise the same skill with the same equipment. For example, you can practise chest passing in pairs with a netball between two;
- All athletes practise the same skill with different equipment, thereby overcoming equipment shortage and catering for different developmental levels. For example, you can get the athletes to work in pairs, some using basketballs, some using netballs to perform ball handling skills;
- All athletes practise the same skill at different levels. For example, in soccer two grids can be used for players heading soccer balls, two grids for heading small soccer balls, and the rest heading with foam balls; and
- Athletes practise different skills in different grids. For example, in two of the grids players can practise passing while stationary, and the athletes in the other grids can practise passing to an open space.

Figure 4.1: A grid

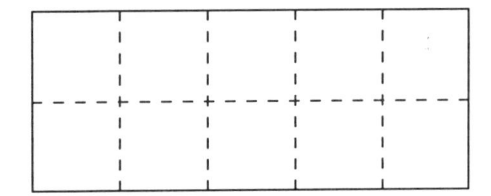

Equipment

As well as planning each training session's learning experiences, you must plan for field/gym space and equipment needs and even have contingencies for something that interrupts your plan. In sport, if there is not enough equipment, athletes do not get enough practise. Keep the equipment well maintained. There is nothing worse than having flat balls or broken beams. A variety of equipment should be available. For example, in cricket, try using harder balls for the more skilled and softer balls for the less skilled, or in batting, the less skilled could practise using a stand (a stationary ball) and the more skilled could practise from a bowl. Equipment can be modified to suit the skill being practised. It is not necessary, for example, to have a particular ball to practise ball handling skills; any type of ball will do. But if it is necessary for athletes to bounce a ball, then it is the coach's responsibility to ensure the balls are filled with air, or if athletes are practising the kinesthetic feel of the ball, then practising with the appropriate ball for the sport is necessary.

ACTIVITY

Maximum opportunity to practise will increase the skill level and the success rate of athletes. You need to ensure that you seek ways to provide maximum opportunity to practise, so when designing your session plans, see if you can provide learning experiences for all levels of skill development. For this activity, observe some other training sessions and look for some new opportunities to enhance the success rate for all your athletes. List some methods that you can use.

What are the equipment needs in your sport? Exchange ideas on how to enhance athlete practice using equipment with other coaches in your sport. Make a list of these ideas.

Point to Ponder
Every child should have a ball with which to practise. If every child has a ball, there will be fewer disruptive children and children will have more chances to improve their skills as they will all have every chance to practise.

Observe some of your own training sessions. If an athlete does not have a piece of equipment to play with or practise on, what is the athlete doing? Is the athlete paying attention? Is the athlete interested in what is going on? Is the athlete helping the other athletes who do have the needed equipment? How long does the athlete stand in line awaiting a turn?

Preparing to Coach the Session

Figure 4.2 is a sample basketball plan for you to work from. There is a blank copy of the plan provided as well. The plan now needs to be prepared. When designing the plan, ask yourself how the material will be presented or, even better, how the athletes will learn this content in the best way. While you design your plan, some useful questions to consider when preparing for the training session are:

- How will you introduce the task? Will you explain it? Demonstrate it? Use questioning?
- How will you know that the athletes understood your instructions?
- What materials or instructional aids will you need to teach the tasks and enable athletes to practise effectively?
- How safe are the tasks and activities that you have planned? Do you need to check equipment?
- Are the progressions of the skill at the athletes' level?

Figure 4.2: An example of a session plan

Session Planner	✓ Things to Remember	Equipment Needed	Training Schedule
Club/School: L.O.O.K. S.H.A.R.P. - Dunedin Sport: Basketball Training Objectives: The players will be able to: 1. demonstrate a basketball stance for defense and ball handling 2. explain 3 key points of a basketball stance 3. communicate positively to team mates and coach	give out newsletter check fitness records	Bibs 1 ball each (12) markers (12)	6-6:10 warm up, stretch 6:10-6:20 Korean passing 6:20-6:30 body fundamental/no ball, jump stop, stride stop, forward, reverse pivot 6:30-6:40 body movement w/ball 6:40-6:50 catch : shoot - drink break - 6:50-7:05 defensive stance 7:05-7:10 pass : cut 7:10-7:20 Add Defense 7:20 3 on 3 7:30 warm down

Injuries

Melanie - ankle

Instructional Methods/Drill and Diagrams

<u>Pass : Cut</u>

key pts -
 hand up for target
 cut towards basket
 replace

<u>Defensive Stance</u>

key pts -
 b/ball position
 drop step
 keep low
 shuffle step

<u>Body Movement - full ct</u>

¼, ½, ¾, full
key teaching pts -
 bent knees
 feet shoulder width
 head up
 back straight
 chest out

<u>Catch : Shoot</u>

partners - 6 baskets
partners pass to each other - 10 shots
from key, outside key, 3 pt line

As you can see from the list of questions, coaching is very complex. The questions listed here are important ones, but don't worry if you are a bit confused about how to demonstrate, explain, question, analyse or provide effective feedback. In Chapters 5, 6 and 7 we will go into more practical applications of these coaching strategies.

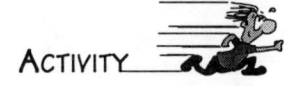

ACTIVITY

Your objectives for a training session plan are prepared. Based on the other information in this chapter, prepare a training session plan. Use the form included at the end of the chapter or design one of your own. Have the plan ready before going on to the self-reflection.

SELF-REFLECTION

After you have designed your training session plan, implement the plan and videotape your training session. If you have not had the opportunity to view yourself on videotape, personally reflect on the training session before proceeding to answer the reflective questions on planning. Remember that you generally go through a self-confrontation phase when viewing yourself on a videotape for the first time. When viewing themselves on videotape, other coaches have often said things like: 'I didn't know that my chin stuck out so far', or 'I didn't know I had such a nose'. This confrontation phase will pass once you become accustomed to viewing *yourself* on the videotape. When comfortable, you will be able to concentrate on aspects of your coaching more effectively.

Evaluate the application of your training plan by answering the following questions when viewing the videotape:

- Did you reach your instructional objectives? Why or why not?
- Were the cue words you chose useful to the athletes? Which, if any, would you change?
- Reflect on your session by answering these questions:
    (a) What did you like best about the session?
    (b) What did you like least about the session?
    (c) How would you improve the session?
- Did all athletes have equal opportunities to practise?
- How well did you plan for different ability levels?
- How well did you plan for use of equipment? Did all athletes have maximum time to practise?

Managing the Environment

There are two main aspects to managing a successful environment for athletes. One is the methods that are used to maintain appropriate behaviour, the other is a learning environment that provides optimal time to practise wisely. A successful learning environment is difficult to define, but it is a responsibility to develop a pleasant environment so that the athletes have the opportunity for optimal learning. Factors that influence the environment include how we 'control' the environment, use equipment, and organise successful and enjoyable training sessions. An important coaching goal is to ensure athletes enjoy their experience and want to come back for more.

Positive Management

As part of developing managing skills, coaches should learn how to ensure appropriate behaviour of athletes so that an optimal learning environment exists. They should develop an environment that allows them to teach and athletes to learn. The managerial element facilitating such an environment establishes the limits and expectations of behaviour of athletes. We often hear about the difficult athlete who causes trouble, seeks attention or is generally disruptive. In developing a positive behavioural environment for learning, remember that the athletes have a right to have a coach who limits disruptive behaviour. Athletes have a right to a coach who provides them with positive support, but also establishes the consequences that will follow inappropriate behaviour. As athlete behaviour is such a concern for coaches, the following section provides suggestions about how to strive for a positive behavioural environment.

Positive management refers to proactive rather than reactive strategies used to develop and maintain a positive, on-task environment in which minimal time is devoted to managerial issues. The positive aspect focuses on the 'good' rather than the 'bad'. An example of positive management is 'Thank you Jo for getting into line the quickest', or 'Well-done Mark, you're sitting and ready to listen'. An example of negative management would be 'Be quiet Frank!' or 'Amanda, get over here!'.

COACHES NEED TO ENSURE AN OPTIMAL LEARNING ENVIRONMENT EXISTS.

For the successful management of athlete behaviour it is essential coaches:

> Reinforce appropriate behaviour.
> Ignore negative behaviour (as much as is safely possible).
> Squelch negative behaviour rather than reinforce it.
> Squelch negative behaviour, reinforce appropriate behaviour.

Look for athletes who are demonstrating appropriate behaviours and praise them. How do you feel when people praise you? How do you feel when people criticise you? Which do you prefer? The positive approach has been researched and proven successful in coach education literature. People prefer praise and positive reinforcement to punishment. In this book we use the term positive management as a method of reinforcing appropriate behaviours.

If coaches do not strive for appropriate athlete behaviour, then by default they are left to disciplining techniques that are unpleasant and create a negative environment. If a training session is run with negative comments or threats of punishment, athletes will participate and strive to *not* make mistakes, rather than strive to learn correctly. Where physical education classes are characterised by negative interactions, student achievement is typically low. The same dynamics apply to coach/athlete interactions.

POINT TO PONDER

Fear of Failure
Remember the coach who used to say, 'If you miss the ball this time, you will run five times around the oval'. You probably tried hard not to miss the ball, but did you try hard to perform the correct technique?

A factor that can be detrimental and frustrating to the smooth flow of the training session is dealing with athletes who are attention seekers. If you acknowledge athletes' appropriate behaviours, you will be giving them positive attention. If you acknowledge their negative behaviours, you will still be giving them attention and reinforcing negative behaviour. The attention received is not determined by whether the behaviour was appropriate or inappropriate, but rather by a simple acknowledgement of the athlete or behaviour.

ACTIVITY

- The first step in positive management is *to define appropriate behaviour*. Appropriate behaviours are all those behaviours that you are willing to accept as part of your training sessions. What athlete behaviours do you accept? Write down your expectations of athletes' behaviours for your team or squad. For example:

Appropriate Behaviours

1. Arrive on time to training.
2. Raise your hand to answer a question.
3. Respect others.
4. Take care of the equipment and facilities and repair breakages.

Your Expected Appropriate Behaviours:

- A second step in positive management is to *define inappropriate behaviours*. When defining inappropriate behaviours be sure to communicate them in a positive way. Once you add the word 'don't' or 'will not', the emphasis is on the negative. For example, if you listed 'The athlete will not talk while I am talking', you would have listed a negative approach. If you list 'The athlete will listen while I am talking', you have set a positive tone. Try defining the inappropriate behaviours you would not expect of your athletes', stating them in a positive fashion.

Inappropriate Behaviours for Your Athletes:

- A third step in positive management is to *emphasise clear expectations and rules* to athletes and parents (we will talk about parents in Chapter 9). Mean what you say and say what you mean. Your expectations must also be consistently enforced. Both rewards and punishments need to be planned. If you tell an athlete that he or she will not compete on Saturday because of poor behaviour, even if that person is your number one athlete, he or she should not compete on Saturday. Be consistent in actioning your expectations with all athletes. If penalties are used, they should be the same for all similar behaviours. See Chapter 5 for further discussion about punishment.
- A fourth step to positive management is to *observe and praise* any of those appropriate behaviours that you see occurring in your training session. Giving praise can be a significant challenge, but if successful, the positive environment created will be conducive to optimal learning and enjoyment. For example, if Peter has been listening attentively, you should acknowledge this by saying something like 'Peter, it is great to see you listening, well done'. Some guidelines to help you provide effective praise are:

  * Provide encouraging comments and gestures to athletes who follow rules. For example, 'I like the way Jane arrives on time to every practice'.

* Set high, yet realistic expectations.
* Give plenty of praise. People thrive on praise. Be sincere in your praising comments and gestures.
* Use effective, positive nonverbal interaction that is compatible with your verbal positive interactions. For example, a smile when praising tells athletes that you were sincere about your praising comment, whereas throwing your hands on your hips and frowning would not provide an encouraging interaction even if your words were positive.
* There is a time and place for public acknowledgement and a time and place where the athletes should be spoken to privately.

- A fifth step in positive management is to *create a plan for decreasing inappropriate behaviour*. To stop an inappropriate behaviour immediately, use effective *desists*. A desist is a verbal cue that reprimands a behaviour. An example of a desist is 'Warren sit down with the rest of the group'. Desists are most effective when combined with a positive management system. For example, if Warren continues to be a problem, you must look for appropriate behaviours he exhibits and praise those. Desists should be clear, be accompanied with firm eye contact, well timed, and well targeted, but not rough, judging or harsh. Try to ignore attention-seeking behaviour. By ignoring behaviour you will eliminate the interaction that provides the reinforcement for attention. If you choose to ignore behaviours as part of your positive management, ensure the environment is safe. If an athlete is being unsafe, stop them immediately.

An environment based on positive management will enhance the opportunities for athletes to learn. Practise these positive management strategies. If you have never actually tried this approach before, it will take time to learn. Athletes will also need to become accustomed to the new you. It is difficult to learn how to be positive, but the benefit of the approach and the look on athletes' faces when they are successful and enjoy the training is well worth the effort. The ultimate goal in positive management is for athletes to have respect for each other and their environment and for you to provide a productive environment.

Managing Time During Training

Time on task is the time that athletes are actually engaged in the required task. It is the time the athletes are practising what they are supposed to be practising. Coaches need to provide high rates of time on task for optimal learning to occur. To maximise time on task, coaches need to plan their sessions to ensure minimal time doing managerial tasks. Managerial tasks are non-instructional tasks that include things like organising teams, gathering athletes for explanations and demonstrations, sending athletes to start the drill, administrative duties (passing out gear, balls), and waiting time (the time athletes wait for their turn).

Non-managerial tasks are those tasks that are related to the task at hand. When you are explaining something about the drill or activity, then it is non-managerial, but if you begin to discuss what happened to the All Whites on the weekend, the instruction is classified as a managerial activity. Feedback about a skill is an example of non-managerial time, however, if you are giving feedback about athletes' behaviour, the activity is classified as managerial. If you tell Martha that her backhand swing is really great, but she needs work on her follow through, then this is considered non-managerial time. If you ask Martha to stop hitting the balls over the fence, then it is considered managerial time. When athletes are actually practising, the activity is non-managerial, but if an athlete is practising the wrong skill the activity is classified as managerial. An example of managerial time is if Lucy is practising a back pike dive and she is supposed to be practising the forward somersault.

Research suggests that if athletes spend more time on the actual physical activity, they will have a higher success rate. Athletes need many opportunities to practise and therefore coaches should maximise the time on task. Factors that increase time on task include providing activities with high participation rates, decreasing instruction time, having appropriate equipment, and reducing the time it takes to move from one activity to another (transition). In Australia and New Zealand, sports tend to provide an average of one hour per week for youth athletes. Within that hour there should be as much opportunity to practise as possible.

ACTIVITY

In the following list, decide which activities are managerial (M) and which are non-managerial (NM).

1. Athletes are asking you to clarify what they are supposed to be doing ___

2. Fiona's parents are talking to you about her uniform ___

3. Alexander is dribbling around the cones and you tell him to switch hands ___

4. You are explaining a drill, then continue to elaborate on the game from Saturday ___

5. You are demonstrating the chest pass ___

6. Scott is playing with the ball while you are explaining the drill and you ask him to stop doing that while you are talking ___

7. You are talking to a parent as the athletes are waiting to start an activity ___

8. You are teaching the freestyle arm stroke using problem-solving and Lisette answers a question you ask about the arm stroke ___

Now that you understand which activities are managerial and non-managerial, you will be able to record the number of minutes that you use as management during your training session. There will be a chance to do this in the self-reflection section. (Answers 1=NM; 2=M; 3=NM; 4=M; 5=NM; 6=M; 7=M; 8=NM.)

Increasing the Amount of Time Athletes Have to Practise

To reach a high level of skill, an athlete should have performed a skill thousands of times, perhaps millions in a lifetime. As suggested earlier, it is important to organise drills so that the athletes have more of an opportunity to practise and perform the skills. The following are strategies that will assist in providing time, within a training session, for athletes to practise.

Routines

One of the ways to increase time on task is to establish organisational routines for the training sessions. For example, do you provide a signal for the athletes to come in for an explanation or demonstration, or do you just call and wait for them to come in? How can you make gathering more efficient? Establish a signal for gathering and dispersing. If such a signal is established, athletes will understand your expectations. For example, when you blow the whistle, athletes are to come to where you are within five seconds.

Another important routine to create is 'how to' distribute equipment. Often coaches have limited budgets and therefore ask their athletes to bring personal equipment. If athletes supply their own equipment, then it is easy to get each one to retrieve theirs quickly. If coaches supply the equipment, then routines to distribute and collect it should be established. For example, select the athletes who are paying attention to go and collect the equipment.

What do the athletes do when they arrive at your training session? Time on task will increase when athletes have routines to follow when they first arrive at training. An example in gymnastics would be to have task cards with warm-up drills for each gymnast. Athletes could be provided with recording sheets to keep track of their progression in these skills. It is important to create activities that do not require a lot of physical exertion as the athletes will not be warmed up. As an alternative, they could warm up and stretch by themselves and be ready to train by a certain time.

Such routines should be established in the first few training sessions of the season. When a drill is being run, practise the routine so that athletes know what to do and what you expect from them. For example, you are in the first training session and the team is practising a dribbling skill. In the middle of the drill, use your gathering signal to see how the athletes respond. Blow your whistle so the athletes can practise coming in quickly. Praise those athletes who do come in quickly to help communicate your expectations.

Prompts and Hustles

Prompts and hustles are cue words to remind athletes what should be done. If these are used when esablishing the routines, it will remind them to quickly complete the managerial task. An example would be 'Huddle', or 'Come in, quickly'. The cue words should encourage quick action. The comments should avoid sarcasm that creates a judging environment, like 'You are slower than your mother'.

Positive Reinforcement

As you may have noted by now, positive reinforcement is essential to establish appropriate behaviours and a positive environment for the athletes to work in. When directing or prompting athletes, coaches should use positive comments to reinforce what was done appropriately, for example, 'Way to go Sarah, you came in quickly', or 'Thank you for picking up the equipment Jason'. The more you positively reinforce those who are doing wonderful things, the smoother the sessions will be.

Flow

To decrease managerial time, a quick-paced or smooth-flowing session is a priority. Try to avoid disruptions or explanations that go off on tangents. Some coaches have fantastic stories, but they should be told before or after training sessions or at team social activities, not during precious training times.

Games

As most sports are competitive in nature, athletes can be encouraged to compete to decrease managerial time. Management tasks can also be fun and somewhat competitive. An example of a management game is:

> *Coach*: Let's play a game to see how quickly you can be ready. When I call you to come in, if you come in within five seconds, you get a point. If you come in after five seconds, I get a point. If you have the most points at the end of the training session, you can choose a game to play. If I have the most points at the end of the training session, I choose what we do.

To increase the amount of time athletes have to practise:

- Have routines that include signals for athletes to come in or start their drills. For example, use the word huddle as a gathering signal for explanations, demonstrations and feedback.
- Use prompts and hustles to encourage quick action.
- Use plenty of positive reinforcement.
- Try to keep a flow going in your session. Try to avoid disruptions or long-winded explanations.
- Make management tasks fun or competitive.

Organising Athletes into Groups

The organisation of athletes into groups creates several issues. Remember the child that for one or the other reason always gets left out? How can we ensure that all athletes are included? There are a multitude of ways to organise athletes into groups. We have to be careful, however, not to hurt athletes' feelings or decrease their self-esteem when organising these groups. There may be a difficult athlete who either has low skill level, or is a behavioural problem, and coaches should consider the most appropriate way to deal with such a person. One way to ensure a feeling of self-esteem for all is to set a system at the beginning of the season so that athletes must say yes to anyone who chooses them as a partner.

One of the quickest ways to select groups or partners is to say "Get a partner", or "get into groups of four". This method generally works quite well with athletes. If this does not work well be sure to have an alternative method to get athletes into small groups. The one difficult area is choosing teams, either for relays or games. In these cases it is useful to use a numbering off system or have the teams listed on your plan. When athletes choose teams, there is invariably someone who usually gets chosen last. This should be avoided.

Activity

There are other more creative ways of getting athletes into groups. For example: 'Those with white shoes go into this team, or those with a last name that is between A and K go into this team'. List creative systems that you use or have seen other coaches use. Observe how other coaches organise their athletes. Observe how other coaches distribute equipment. List some of these organising systems that you can use.

Self-Reflection

For this exercise you will need to have several training sessions of your coaching available on videotape. Answer the questions before you develop your managing skills and then again after you begin to develop your managing skills, for a comparison. There are two things to look for in your coaching: the first is the use of positive management; and the second is the amount of time that athletes actually practise. The following are reflective questions about your coaching.

Positive Management

- How many positive comments for appropriate behaviours did you make? Were you happy with the ratio of positive to negative comments?
- Did you notice any effect on the athletes who were praised?
- How many desists did you give? Were they necessary? Why or why not? Did they work?

- Were you consistent in communicating those expectations as were listed in the appropriate and inappropriate behaviour activity?
- Did you learn anything about your positive management this session?
- Did you learn anything about your athletes' behaviours?
- Where do you think the training session could be improved?

Increasing Time on Task

- What percentage of time did you spend in managerial tasks?
- Were you happy with the amount of time that the athletes were able to practise for this session? Why or why not?
- Get a spectator to observe one athlete during your session and record the number of times the athlete performed using the equipment. How much time did the athlete spend waiting for his or her turn? Were you happy with this? Why or why not?
- What will help you decrease your management time?
- Write down the names of the athletes on your team and tick after their name each time you give them feedback. Were you able to give equal feedback to everyone on your team?

Summary

1. Planning is important for providing quality learning experiences for athletes and ensuring a smooth flow to your training sessions.
2. The first step to planning is to establish instructional objectives for the training session. These objectives should include the performance, cognitive and affective learning domains.
3. Performance objectives are those that relate to movement skills. Cognitive objectives are those that relate to knowledge about tactics, strategies, rules and skills. Affective objectives are those that relate to attitudes and values.
4. Objectives should be written as outcomes and describe the task to be learned, the situations under which the task will be performed and the criteria in which the task outcomes will be measured.
5. Based on your objectives, identify the main tasks to be learned and the subtasks that are required to perform each main task.
6. A task analysis is a chain of subtasks that lead to the terminal task performance. A task analysis helps to make a decision on the instructional process to use in teaching the skills, knowledge or behaviour.
7. Cue words of tasks and subtasks can remind coaches of teaching points.
8. Planning requires a consideration of different ability levels, the organisation of drills, equipment and instructional aids, safety implications and appropriate progression of skills.
9. There are two aspects to managing an effective learning environment: maintaining appropriate behaviour and providing optimal time on task.
10. Positive management involves reinforcing appropriate behaviour and ignoring negative behaviour.

11. When a negative training environment pervades, athletes' achievement is low.
12. A managerial task is a non-instructional episode which includes organising athletes, gathering and dispersing athletes and time athletes spend waiting. A non-managerial task is an episode that is related to instruction.
13. To increase time on task, coaches should plan routines to decrease time in organisational matters such as gathering and dispersing athletes, arranging groups, distributing equipment or listening to the coach.

Further Reading

Christina, R.W. and Corcas, D.M. (1988), *Coaches Guide to Teaching Sport Skills*, Champaign, IL: Human Kinetics.

Feltz, D.L. and Weiss, M.R. (1982), 'Developing Self-efficacy through Sport', *Journal of Physical Education, Recreation and Dance*, vol. 53, no. 3, pp. 24–26.

Graham, G., Holt/Hale, S., Parker, M. (1993), *Children Moving: A Reflective Approach to Teaching Physical Education*, Palo Alto, CA: Mayfield Publishing.

Graham, G. (1992), *Teaching Physical Education: Becoming a Master Teacher*, Champaign, IL: Human Kinetics.

Randall, L. (1992), *Systematic Supervision for Physical Education*, Champaign, IL: Human Kinetics.

Siedentop, D. (1991), *Developing Teaching Skills in Physical Education*, Mountain View, CA: Mayfield.

Thompson, J. (1993), *Positive Coaching*, Portola Valley, CA: Warde.

Figure 4.2: An example of a session plan

Session Planner	Things to Remember	Equipment Needed	Training Schedule

Club/School:
Sport:
Training Objectives:

Injuries

Instructional Methods/Drill and Diagrams

Chapter 5

Creating a Positive Environment

- Positive Approach
- Communication
- Motivation

There are numerous facets to a positive environment, some of which have been mentioned in Chapter 4. Before detailing what coaches can do to be positive, communicate effectively and enhance the motivation of their athletes, we will first briefly identify five other important facets of a positive environment. The environment is:

1. *Supportive* – a positive environment offers accessible support when needed. Support can come in many forms. Positive reinforcement can increase athletes' self-worth and feelings of competence. There is informational support in the form of advice or suggestions. Tangible or instrumental support can be in the form of equipment, transportation or facilities. Social support provides affiliation and feelings of self-worth. A lack of social support, although undesirable, is not the worst case scenario. Even worse than no social support is the presence of social disapproval. Ridicule indisputably has a negative impact on individuals. Disapproval, whether demonstrated by the silent treatment, sarcasm or outright rage, is obviously not present in a positive environment.
2. *Allows self-determination* – self-determination was mentioned in Chapter 1 as a major component of intrinsic motivation. If athletes are placed in an environment where they are always told what to do, when to do it and how to do it, they fail to learn to think for themselves. When athletes have some sense of input or control, not only do they increase their awareness, their ability to think and make decisions, they also feel less manipulated and therefore, learn to take responsibility for their actions.
3. *Familiar yet challenging* – familiarity is good in that it is comfortable and athletes know what to expect. However, when things become too familiar (for example always doing the same drills in the same order), boredom sets in. New situations and new experiences provide challenge.

82 The Coaching Process

A POSITIVE ENVIRONMENT IS A SAFE ENVIRONMENT.

4. *Safe* – the environment should always be structured in a way that minimises injury and harm. Attention should be paid to surfaces, equipment, protective clothing/equipment as well as correct technique, warm up, etc.
5. *Allows for individual differences* – when athletes know that it is okay to be different and that they do not have to be exactly like everyone else, it gives them the freedom to explore and try new things as well as allows their self-esteem and self-concept to originate with themselves, rather than how they compare to others. Also, exposure to a variety of people can enhance the acceptance and appreciation of people who are different to oneself.

Positive Approach

Because of individual differences in both athletes and coaches, no single prescriptive approach to coaching will be equally effective in all situations. However, even with the individualisation of coaching approaches, an emphasis on the positive is warranted. It has been suggested that a basic ratio of four positives for every negative is effective, but even more emphasis should be placed on the positive when first working with a person or team or when introducing a new skill or strategy. If you are not sure how positive to be, at first err on the side of being too positive, then later adjust to individual and situational requirements.

What is the Positive Approach?

The positive approach is more than just telling your athletes that they are wonderful. The positive approach is a combination of providing information and rewards while being sincere and realistic.

Rewards are an important aspect of the positive approach. Coaches should reward and encourage their athletes both verbally and nonverbally. Very rarely are rewards such as money, trophies, or other tangible objects needed. However, over-reliance on any one form of verbal or nonverbal encouragement can limit its value. Therefore, using a variety of verbal and nonverbal forms of reinforcement is ideal.

ACTIVITY

Provide five additional examples of verbal and nonverbal encouragement. (Remember to use a pencil or photocopy the activity.)

Verbal	Nonverbal
1. 'Well done!'	1. Thumbs up
2.	2.
3.	3.
4.	4.
5.	5.
6.	6.

It is important to be sincere when giving rewards or encouragement. An insincere or sarcastic 'well done' is obviously not part of the positive approach. Rewards should be given immediately and contingently. It is no good saying, 'That kick of yours two weeks ago was well controlled'. To be effective the reinforcement needs to be given only when deserved and then as soon as possible.

Unfortunately it is usually outcomes and results that get rewarded. A concerted effort should be made to reinforce technique, performance, effort and other factors that the athlete can control. Athletes cannot control outcomes. If Sharon is swimming in lane 4, she can only control what happens in lane 4. She has no control over what happens in lanes 1, 2, 3, 5, 6, 7 or 8. Similarly, in softball Earl cannot control what everyone else on his team does. Coaches can reward technique, effort, punctuality or encouragement of a team mate.

Another aspect of the positive approach is to have realistic expectations of your athletes. If Jane currently swims the 50 m free in 45 seconds, focus on her improving her performance to 44 or 43 seconds. Or better still, focus on developing techniques that will help her have a stronger kick or a more efficient pull. Some coaches argue that they do not want to restrain their athletes by limiting expectations in any way and thus expect that their athletes can do anything and everything. Expectations that are unrealistic, however, only serve to set athletes up for failure. Expecting Jane to be able to swim the 50m free in 30 seconds would probably result in her complaining, dropping out and/or developing very low self-esteem.

Similarly, telling Bob that he has great potential as a sailer is not always a positive move. Potential can become a very heavy weight for an individual to carry. If Bob believes that he continually fails to reach his 'potential', he will probably lose confidence, not only in himself, but also in his coach and his training programme. Each error he makes becomes an example to him of how he is a failure.

Positive coaches respond to errors in a positive manner. Positive instruction is sometimes called 'sandwich instruction' or 'CRC instruction'. Basically, CRC instruction involves sandwiching the instruction between two positives. CRC stands for 'Commend, Recommend, Commend'. The first step is to commend or compliment the athlete. The second step is to recommend what should be done differently (give instruction) and the third and final step is to commend again by giving another positive assertion or a statement of encouragement.

Example: Giving positive instruction for an athlete working on backcourt skills in volleyball:

Commend: 'Good try, you read the ball well'
Recommend: 'Next time, be down low when the ball is hit'
Commend: 'You've almost got it!'

ACTIVITY

Provide two examples of sandwich or CRC instruction for common errors made by athletes in your sport:

Commend:
Recommend:
Commend:

Commend:
Recommend:
Commend:

An important aspect of correcting errors is to state the correction, recommendation, or instruction in positive terms. Coaches can be very enthusiastic and supportive of their athletes, but then reduce their effectiveness by wording statements negatively. For example, a common error in beginning backstrokers is that they bend their arms during the recovery phase of the stroke (when the arm is out of the water). The automatic inclination is to tell them not to bend their arms. As coaches we quickly see that something is being done incorrectly, and instinctively tell athletes not to do it. Instead, we should take the extra bit of time and work our brains a bit harder and tell them what it is that *we want* them to do.

POINT TO PONDER
Don't think of pink elephants! When this statement is made, what is the first thing that comes into your mind?

If athletes are told "Don't bend your arms", the first thing they think about is bending their arms. Some athletes will actually picture themselves bending their arms and will therefore be mentally practising exactly what you do not want them to do. Thus the instruction to keep their arms straight, rather than not to bend their arms, gives them a positive visual image to focus on.

ACTIVITY

Reword the following instructions so they are phrased positively, focusing the athletes' attention on the desired behaviour.

Don't bend your elbow.	Keep your arm straight.
Don't serve into the net.	_____
Don't have your weight on your heels.	_____
Don't drop the ball.	_____
Whatever you do, don't false start.	_____

SELF-REFLECTION

Videotape yourself for an hour during a training session. Play the tape back and count the number of times you worded something in the negative. For every negatively worded statement, write down how it could have been stated in the positive.

Why Use the Positive Approach?

The positive approach does not guarantee winning. However, the positive approach to coaching does influence athletes' attitudes. It should come as no surprise that coaches who use more reinforcement, encouragement and instruction and fewer punitive behaviours are liked better and are seen as better teachers than coaches who are more negative. Athletes with positive coaches also like the sport and their team mates more than do athletes with negative coaches. In addition, athletes with positive coaches express a greater desire to continue participating in their sport and overall genuinely enjoy taking part.

What about Punishment?

Punishment is sometimes necessary to temporarily stop detrimental behaviour. Reinforcement does not always work perfectly by itself. Therefore, coaches need to be able to use punishment effectively. Punishment is most often called for when athletes' behaviour is dangerous to themselves or others. When the following guidelines are followed, punishment can be part of the positive approach (although just a small part).

- Use punishment in a corrective manner to stop a behaviour. It is the behaviour that is being punished, not the person. Once the punishment has been served, the athlete is back on equal footing with everyone else.
- Be impersonal when punishing. Punishment should be imposed calmly. When coaches yell or use comments that belittle an individual, the punishment can easily be perceived as revenge or a desperate attempt by the coach to show who is in charge.
- Be consistent across time and across athletes. Everyone should receive the same type of punishment for breaking similar rules. Similarly, if a particular behaviour is punished early in the season, the same behaviour should be punished later in the season.
- Be careful in the selection of punishments. If you use a punishment that makes you feel guilty, that guilt will overshadow your relationship with the athlete far into the future. Be sure the punishment you select is actually perceived as punishment and not a reinforcer. For example, when an athlete is made to sit out of a drill for being disruptive, the athlete may perceive that as a reinforcer if the particular drill is disliked.
- Never use physical activity as a punishment. Although very effective in the short term, using physical activity as punishment sends a message that physical activity or exercise is unpleasant, something to be avoided and something only to be endured when one has been bad.

Communication

As a coach, having all the knowledge in the world about your sport is worthless to your athletes if it cannot be communicated to them. If coaches want athletes to listen over time, they cannot deliver their messages with sarcasm or threats. Making negative comparisons of your athletes with others is also a good way of ensuring that they will stop listening (or stop coming to training altogether). Using the positive approach, however, is only a small part of effective communication.

Creating a Positive Environment 87

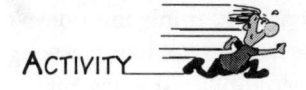

ACTIVITY

For each of the following scenarios, determine the aspect(s) of communication that could make the coach more effective. What should each coach do to be more effective?

1. Rodney knows a lot about his sport and tries to get all that information across to his athletes at every opportunity. As a result, his athletes are often overloaded with information.

2. Judy is concerned about hurting the feelings of her athletes. So, when she has to drop people from her team she tries to maintain their self-confidence by telling them that they are in fact quite skilled or dedicated. These athletes end up being confused – why were they dropped if they are so good?

3. Mark is coaching his child's team because he felt that if he didn't, no one else would. He doesn't really know that much about the sport and without realising it often says things that aren't quite right.

4. Vanessa expects her athletes to be on time to training, follow good nutritional advice and get plenty of sleep. She is often found rushing to morning training sessions while munching on a pastry and looking as if she just woke up.

5. Ken used to compete in the top level of his sport. He is now coaching a team of novices and often uses terminology (jargon) that they don't understand.

6. Ashley feels she gives her athletes lots of feedback. She is constantly telling them when they are performing well and when their performance just isn't good enough. The athletes are getting frustrated because they don't know what they should do to improve.

7. Justin provides his team with useful information and carefully plans his training sessions. His athletes, however, feel that he is unapproachable and that he doesn't understand how they feel.

8. Jan is worried that her team doesn't respect her and that they think she doesn't know what she is talking about. Therefore, she never admits to being wrong because she feels that if she did she would lose whatever credibility she has left.

Now, using the aspects of communication you listed above, write down your own communication strengths and weaknesses.

Strengths	Weaknesses

Two aspects of communication that coaches usually need to work on the most are their nonverbal communication skills and their listening skills. Nonverbal aspects of communication (or body language) include mannerisms, movements, touching behaviours, voice characteristics, how much space you allow between yourself and others, body positions (for example arms crossed in front) and facial expressions.

Nonverbal skills can become even more important when talking one on one with athletes. ROLL with your athletes.

R Remain relatively *RELAXED* with your athletes as you interact with them. This indicates your confidence in what you are doing and helps them relax.

O Face your athletes and adopt an *OPEN* posture. This says that you are available to work with them and that you are non-defensive.

L *LEAN* towards the athletes at times. This emphasises your attentiveness.

L *LOOK* at your athletes when communicating with them. Maintaining eye contact without staring shows that you are interested in them and their concerns.

ROLLING.

Creating a Positive Environment   89

Activity

Get together with two other people who are interested in enhancing their communication skills. Take turns playing the roles of coach, athlete (or parent of an athlete) and an observer. Have the athlete (or parent of an athlete) relate to the coach his or her goals and expectations of her or his (or the child's) participation in sport. After two or three minutes have the observer give the coach feedback about how well they ROLLed with the other person. Try to identify something that was excellent and something else that could be improved. After the observer has given feedback, then allow the athlete (or parent of the athlete) to comment. Be sure each person gets an opportunity to play each role.

As mentioned above, the other communication skill in need of improvement by most coaches is the ability to listen. Usually coaches are very good at jumping straight into a situation and giving advice. Unfortunately, when people go directly into advice giving mode, they often do so without being entirely clear on the situation. Listening is a greatly underrated skill.

Activity

To begin to reflect on your listening skills, for the following scenarios, indicate the key experience, behaviours and feelings or emotions generated by the person. An example is not provided as that would suggest that there is a single correct response to each scenario. Just make your best judgement.

A. An athlete in her teens is concerned about her levels of anxiety during major competitions. She has always performed really well at the local level, but national and international competition scares her.

Key experience	
Key behaviours	
Feelings or emotions generated	

B. An athlete in his mid-20s has been married a little over a year. He has just quit work to train full time. He is having trouble with his marriage. He is having second thoughts about quitting his job and training full time.

Key experience	
Key behaviours	
Feelings or emotions generated	

C. A 16-year-old athlete, who has been told she has great potential, is feeling really stressed because she wants to do as well as possible in sport. She realises that a career in sport can be relatively short and therefore wants to be sure to gain entrance into a university. She does not know if she can keep training as much as expected and still get the grades in school that she needs to be able to study at a university.

Key experience	
Key behaviours	
Feelings or emotions generated	

By trying to determine the key experience, behaviours and emotions the emphasis is on understanding the specific situation rather than solving problems. In many instances the athletes themselves are not entirely clear about what the issue is. By trying to clarify the situation for yourself, you may in fact help the athlete clarify it for him or herself. If you compare your responses to the above scenarios with somebody else's responses, you will probably find a few differences. This inconsistency does not mean that either of you is wrong. Often the situation that is first presented to us lacks clarity.

The next step is to communicate your understanding of the situation to the athlete concerned. If your understanding is correct, communication will be enhanced as the athlete will believe you really grasp what she or he is experiencing. If your initial understanding is incorrect, communication will be enhanced by the athlete clarifying the situation. Your sincere attempt to understand what the athletes are experiencing will encourage them to clarify the situation.

ACTIVITY

For the next scenarios, list two different ways in which you would try to express understanding to the individual involved. An example is provided.

A parent is concerned that her child will get hurt participating in sport at the more advanced level. The child is talented, but the parent feels that the child's health and safety are more important than any performance.

1. "You are worried that if your child keeps competing he'll get hurt."
2. "You believe that it is better for your child to stay at the lower level than to compete at a more advanced level where there is a greater chance he might get hurt."

D. A fellow coach is losing sleep because he can't make the final decision about which athletes to include in his representative team. He has selected the bulk of his team, but the final two spaces are down to four athletes. He spends all his time weighing the pros and cons of each of these four athletes and how they would fit in the team. He's incredibly stressed about it.

1.

2.

E. An athlete you coach approaches you to complain that you treat the star player differently than you do everyone else. This top athlete gets away with being late to training and missing some training sessions entirely. Nothing is said when this happens, but if anyone else did the same thing they'd get pulled up in front of the whole team.

1.

2.

F. The administrative body of your sport demands to know why your athletes have not been more successful. They believe that with the talent you have available to you, you should have obtained more impressive results.

1.

2.

It was probably more difficult to come up with expressions of understanding in the last two scenarios. Two things need to be stated here. First of all, communicating that you understand what someone else is experiencing is not the same thing as agreeing with the person. Second, demonstrating that you understand what the other person is experiencing in a confrontational situation can help diffuse anger and therefore increase the chances of eventually dealing effectively with the situation.

Listening and understanding are the first two requirements for effective communication. If either of these steps is skipped, any actions that follow may be less than ideal. Instead of immediately justifying your own behaviour or doling out advice, first be entirely clear about the situation.

Motivation

Sometimes coaches complain that a particular athlete is not motivated or they worry about the decreased motivation of an entire team. Motivation is a commonly used term, but is not necessarily an entirely understood concept. There are very few unmotivated people. It might be problematic for coaches who have athletes who are motivated to play video games or go to the movies instead of going to training, but the individuals themselves are not devoid of motivation.

Before continuing this discussion, it is useful to consider what motivation actually is. Motivation is made up of three components: direction, intensity and persistence. Direction refers to where we choose to invest our energy. You may choose to go to the movies, the opera, training, or home. We all have lots of choices when it comes to direction. If you want your athletes to choose the direction of training, you might consider how to make training inviting and enjoyable.

The second aspect of motivation is intensity. Intensity refers to how much effort an individual puts into the chosen direction. You have probably experienced the situation where many athletes have chosen the direction of training, but they participate at different levels of intensity. Most coaches want their athletes to try hard at training and feel that the more intensity athletes demonstrate at training, the better. Too much intensity, however, may have a negative impact on the third component of motivation, persistence.

Persistence is sticking with something over time. Sometimes when athletes train with high levels of intensity they experience problems with staleness, overtraining or burnout. Too much intensity may lead to quitting. If we want our athletes to persist, we need to be careful about maintaining appropriate levels of intensity. More is not always better. If your athletes are tired, irritable, having a drop off in performance, getting sick or just looking bored, the intensity level may be too high.

Increasing Enjoyment

As mentioned above, making training sessions enjoyable will increase the chance of athletes choosing the direction of training. Similarly, just as coaches can be intrinsically motivated to coach, athletes can be intrinsically motivated to train. Remember that intrinsically motivated behaviours are those behaviours that a person engages in to feel competent and self-determining. Coaches can enhance athletes' intrinsic motivation by allowing them opportunities to feel competent and self-determining.

Structuring the environment so there is a reasonable probability of success can increase athletes' feelings of competence. By matching task difficulty with ability levels, drills can be organised to meet the needs of the individuals (see Chapter 4). If the drill is too difficult, athletes will perceive themselves to be failures, causing intrinsic motivation to decrease. On the other hand, if the drill is too easy, intrinsic motivation is not enhanced because successful completion of a simple task does not indicate competence.

Activity

Select two drills commonly used in your sport. Describe how you could make each task easier or more difficult so that it could be matched to the ability levels of individuals.

Drill	Easy Version	Difficult Version

Feelings of competence can also be influenced by increasing each athlete's perceived significance to the team. When athletes have clearly defined roles, they are more likely to recognise their contributions to the team. These roles should be openly discussed.

Intrinsic motivation can also be enhanced by letting the athletes make some decisions. They might decide what time training will be, how long training will last, or what drills might be done. This strategy relates to the self-determination aspect of intrinsic motivation.

Self-determination can also be increased by allowing experienced athletes to have input into what strategies or tactics will be used in a particular competition. Players can also feel empowered by leading some segments of training. For example, they might take turns leading warm up or running particular drills.

Individuals are more likely to choose directions that they feel will give them what they want. Therefore, it is imperative to focus on their reasons and motives for participating in sport. If they are primarily involved because they want to play with their friends, then dividing a large group into ability levels that causes them to be separated from their friends would decrease their enjoyment. It is worth discovering the motives of your athletes (see Chapter 3).

Lastly, enjoyment will be increased by making participation fun. Avoid specialising players into positions or roles at an early age. Let participants play different positions and try different skills. Fun might also be experienced if they train in a different place, learn something other kids don't know, play music at training, try something a bit daring, have a chance to really scream and yell, get a special treat, or play games.

Activity

Ask your athletes what they think is fun during training. Record the 10 most popular answers on the left side of the following form. Then decide how you can incorporate their ideas of fun into training or competition on the right side of the form.

What is Fun	How to Include It
1.	
2.	
3.	
4.	
5.	
6.	
7.	
8.	
9.	
10.	

Goal Setting

Why Set Goals?

A very effective technique for maintaining or enhancing motivation is goal setting. Setting goals can enhance all three components of motivation: direction, intensity and persistence. Goals give direction by providing a target; people can see what they are aiming for, what they are trying to achieve.

Goals enhance intensity in that they provide reasons for our behaviour. When you are asked to do something that you believe has no value or purpose, it is likely that you will not put much effort into that activity. Athletes find value in completing drills that they believe can help them achieve their goals. Similarly, coaches find value in actively changing how they coach if they believe it will help them achieve their goals. We all put more effort into activities that we believe serve a purpose. Intensity levels increase when we are striving to achieve goals rather than just going through the motions of coaching or training.

> **POINT TO PONDER**
> 'My motivation was to consistently attain the standards of excellence I set for myself'
> (Greg Chappell)

Goals also help with the persistence component of motivation. Persistence is aided in two ways by goals: (1) reinforcement for success and (2) perseverance when success is not readily achieved. Achieving goals makes us feel that what we are doing is valuable. We are more likely to continue doing something when we feel that by doing so we will achieve what we want. Reaching goals increases our confidence and gives our motivation an extra boost. If, on the other hand, we have a goal that we are struggling to achieve, we will persist by finding new strategies if we believe the goal to be worthwhile. If we really want to attain a particular goal, we will find additional methods or ways of helping ourselves. If there is no goal, however, we will likely quit. Unfortunately, although many athletes and coaches set goals, they do so in a manner that is not as effective as it could be.

Long-term and Short-term Goals

One common problem in goal setting is that people set only long-term goals. At times, a long-term goal can seem so far away, that the individual gives up before getting there. A series of short-term goals that lead to the long-term goal can provide reinforcement along the way. Once the first short-term goal is achieved, individuals will have improved self-confidence and motivation which will in turn encourage their achievement of the next short-term goal. Without the attainment of short-term goals, people don't get the message that what they are doing is working. It is very difficult to maintain motivation towards a task when the benefits of doing so are questionable.

Controllable Goals

Setting a series of short-term goals with the final aim of achieving a long-term goal is only one aspect of goal setting. In addition, goals need to be related to performance or technique rather than outcomes. If individuals set goals related to an outcome (e.g. winning), then they will be thinking about the outcome rather than what it is they need to do to achieve the outcome they want. Winning is great fun, almost everyone enjoys winning. But, if we focus on nothing other than winning we actually will be decreasing our chances of winning. You have probably seen examples of athletes or teams who have been focused on outcomes, been noticeably ahead during the competition, thought they had it won, slackened off on their own performance only to be beaten at the very end. Similarly, performance decreases when athletes have an outcome goal and perceive that winning is not possible. The thinking then seems to go along the lines of, 'Well, I can't win, so I might as well give up'.

> POINT TO PONDER
> 'Further decreasing my times was the major incentive for me to do well'
>
> (Shane Gould Innes)

Setting outcome goals is also problematic for other reasons. Using swimming as an example, if all swimmers in an event had the goal of winning, everyone would have failed except for the one person who won. Even a swimmer with a personal best time who came in second would be a failure if the only goal was to win. Each swimmer can only control what happens in her or his own lane. Performance or technique goals encourage swimmers (and in fact all athletes) to focus on what they can control.

Coaches need to remember that their goals should also be controllable. It is easy to fall into the trap of setting the goal of having athletes you coach being selected for representative teams. This is an example of an outcome goal. You cannot control it. Not only does it rely on the politics of your sporting organisation, it also relies on what your athletes will do. Setting goals that require other people to do things is immediately putting the achievement of the goals outside your control.

Challenging but Realistic Goals

Effective goal setting also requires that a balance be achieved between challenge and realism. Some individuals are so concerned about succeeding and being able to say that they achieved their goals, that the goals they set are actually deeds they can currently achieve. They are guaranteed to achieve their goals, but doing so will not enhance their performance or change their behaviour in any way. Other individuals tend to go to the opposite extreme. They feel that setting realistic goals is restrictive and argue that by expecting the impossible from themselves they avoid setting any limits on themselves. Although technically this may be true, in reality they usually just end up setting themselves up for failure. Continual failure to achieve goals often results in decreased motivation, decreased self-confidence and decreased confidence in the programme and those around them.

Positive Goals

Identical to the procedure of correcting errors as part of the positive approach of coaching, it is necessary to state goals in positive terms. If goals are worded in the negative, individuals are thinking about, planning for and possibly doing exactly what it is that they do not want. Phrasing goals in the positive encourages people to think about, plan for and finally achieve what they desire.

Specific and Measurable Goals

A common error in goal setting is being too vague about what it is one wants to accomplish. Setting the goal of being a better coach, a fitter athlete, or a more knowledgeable individual does not allow the person to know if or when success has been achieved. For goals to be effective they need to be specific and measurable. The easiest way to do this is to make them numerical.

For goals where objective measures such as distances, weights, repetitions or times cannot be used, using previously established subjective rating scales may be beneficial. For example, if someone tends to be very negative and is always swearing and remembering past mistakes instead of being positive and constructive, setting a goal of increasing positive and constructive self-talk would be useful but virtually impossible to measure objectively. Creating a subjective 10-point rating scale where 'one' means the person's self-talk was entirely negative and 'ten' means the person's self-talk was entirely positive and constructive is a means of trying to make subjective goals more measurable. Of course it is important to define all the numbers on the scale, not just the endpoints. If the numbers are not defined prior to working towards the goal, it often results in the scale changing as the behaviour changes, with behaviour that was originally rated as 'six' being rated as 'three'.

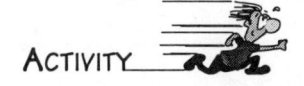

ACTIVITY

Restate the following goals in terms that are specific and measurable and remain positive.

Vague Goal	Specific Goal
I want to be faster in the 100m sprint.	I want to improve my personal best in the 100 m sprint by two seconds.
I want to be a more consistent scorer in basketball.	
I want to have a tougher serve in volleyball.	
I want to improve the planning of my training sessions.	

Often when athletes and coaches are told that outcome goals are to be avoided, they have difficulty determining useful performance or technique goals. Goals can be set in a variety of areas. Athletes can set goals in the areas of physical fitness (strength, power, speed, flexibility, endurance, agility), physical technique (dependent on the sport), mental skills (for example, self-confidence, arousal control, imagery, concentration, or self-talk), tactics and strategies, general health (for example, nutrition and sleep), as well as numerous other domains such as attendance at training, being on time, looking after equipment and communicating with others. Although coaches may want to set similar goals as athletes (particularly in relation to stress or time management), they might also consider the areas of knowledge, planning and management of training sessions and instructional techniques.

ACTIVITY

A bit of thinking and introspection is required for individuals to set appropriate goals. Using whatever reference points you choose, answer the following questions:

A. Where are you now (where do you see yourself as a coach)?

B. Where do you want to be in one month (again, in reference to coaching, as opposed to 'on a beach in Tahiti')?

C. Where do you want to be in six months? What changes would you like to see in your own coaching?

D. Where do you want to be in two years (allow yourself to dream a little bit)?

E. List three strengths and three weaknesses you have as a coach (remember, these can relate to any area of your coaching performance):

Strengths	Weaknesses
1.	1.
2.	2.
3.	3.

F. Review what you have written above. Now select an area that you want to work on. Some coaches choose to strengthen one of their weaknesses, others choose to take greater advantage of one of their strengths. This is your choice. It is also possible to refer back to something you wrote in terms of where you want to be in the future.

G. In the area that you have chosen, set a long-term goal with a target date. By long term, think along the lines of what you want to achieve in your selected area in the next six months to two years. When you write the target date, be sure to write the actual date. Many individuals make the mistake of saying, 'In one year I will achieve X'. The problem arises when six months down the track they reread their goal and it still says, 'In one year ...'.

H. Once you have set your long-term goal, set a series of short-term goals that will lead you to it. Use the time frame of one to four weeks for your short-term goals. You may find it helpful to consider the short-term goals as a staircase to get you where you want to go. At the moment you are at the bottom of the stairs. Each short-term goal is a step that brings you closer to the top of the stairs (your long-term goal).

I. Check that your short-term goals (particularly the first one) are challenging, realistic, positive, specific, measurable and controllable and that they have target dates. If your goals do not meet these requirements, rewrite them so they do.

J. Some people make the error of thinking they have completed the goal-setting process at this point, but they have failed to determine what they are going to do to achieve their goals. Strategies need to be outlined for achieving the short-term goals. Ideas and suggestions from others are very useful at this point. Gather together at least four strategies that could be used to aid the achievement of your first short-term goal. You may not use all the strategies, but it is always useful to have a backup in case the original plan doesn't work.

1.

2.

3.

4.

Now it is time to get even more specific. What exactly are you going to do during the next two weeks that will help you achieve your goal. Be sure to address when, where and how you will be applying your strategy(ies).

Goals must be evaluated on a regular basis. It does you no good to outline specific goals, target dates and strategies just to find them buried under a pile of magazines six months later. When the target date for a short term goal arrives, evaluate whether or not you have achieved the goal. If you have, great! Celebrate! Often the achievement of the goal is reward enough in and of itself, but you may want to reward yourself with a special treat. Achieving the goal will give you belief in your strategies and maintain or enhance your confidence and motivation which you then need to apply to the next goal (the next step).

If, however, the target date arrives and you have not achieved your goal, there is no need to commit hara-kiri. Instead, reflect on why the goal was not achieved. Perhaps you got sick, injured or bogged down with work and were unable to make progress towards your goal. So set a new target date. Perhaps the size of the step was too big. In that case, set a new, more realistic short-term goal with a new target date. You may still believe the goal to be a good one, but the strategy you selected was ineffective. Set a new target date, but then apply different strategies.

For goal setting to be most effective, the goals need to be recorded in a manner that allows you to remind yourself on a regular basis what it is you are trying to achieve. You might record the goals in a training diary or planner and when recording or planning, be reminded of your goals. Alternatively, you might record your goals onto a cassette (with background music if you like) and then play the cassette in a personal stereo (Walkman) either before going to sleep or while on your way to training or competition. Another possibility is to make a poster of your goal, where you can shade in your improvement or achievements as you go. Some individuals choose to display these posters in a public place (such as the changing room) because they believe making their goal public will be added motivation for them. Others, however, would see the public display of their goals as a source of unneeded pressure and therefore prefer to keep their goals private.

The goal-setting process outlined above is very effective, but often athletes and coaches need to be thinking about achieving goals in more than one area. Using a form such as the one that follows can be useful. The example provided is designed for athletes. 'Other' can refer to study, work, or other commitments outside of sport that can distract or disrupt sporting involvement if not dealt with. The categories can be changed if the form is to be used with coaches.

Goal	Target Date	Strategies
Fitness		
Technique		
Mental		
Other		

Remember, this goal-setting process is useful for both athletes and coaches. You can lead your athletes through a similar process to that listed above. Keep in mind, however, that the athletes need to set their own goals. Setting goals for them may be simpler, easier and less time consuming for you, but the athletes will have much more commitment and energy for goals they set themselves. Coaches, however, can be a very good source of ideas for strategies. It is imperative to recognise that the goal setting process is exactly that, a process. Just sitting down once at the beginning of the season and setting a few goals does not mean that you can tick 'goals' off your list of things to do. Goals need to be continually revisited.

Summary

1. A positive environment is supportive, allows self-determination, is familiar yet challenging, is safe and allows for individual differences.
2. The positive approach is a combination of providing information and rewards while being sincere and realistic.
3. Encouragement can be verbal and nonverbal.
4. Errors should be corrected in a positive manner: Commend, Recommend, Commend.
5. All instructions should be phrased positively.
6. Coaches need to be able to communicate effectively with their athletes.
7. Nonverbal communication skills can be improved by ROLLing with your athletes: be Relaxed, have an Open posture, Lean towards them and Look at them.
8. Listening and understanding are the first two requirements for effective communication. Most coaches need to improve their listening skills.
9. Motivation is made up of direction, intensity and persistence.
10. Athletes are likely to choose the direction of training if they have a reasonable probability of experiencing success, they feel they have some input into the programme and training is fun.
11. An effective technique for maintaining or enhancing motivation is goal setting.
12. Athletes and coaches should set controllable, challenging but realistic, positive, specific and measurable goals.
13. Goals need to have target dates and strategies and should be evaluated on a regular basis.

Further Reading

Martens, R. (1987), *Coaches' Guide to Sport Psychology*, Champaign, IL: Human Kinetics.

Winter, G. (1995), 'Goal Setting', in Morris, T. and Summers, J. (eds), *Sport Psychology: Theory, Applications and Issues,* Brisbane: John Wiley and Sons, pp. 259–270.

Yukelson, D. (1993), 'Communicating Effectively', in Williams, J.M. (ed.), *Applied Sport Psychology: Personal Growth to Peak Performance,* Mountain View, CA: Mayfield, pp. 122–136.

Chapter 6

Instructional Techniques

- Demonstrations
- Explanations
- Questioning

Do you remember the teacher you had when you were in high school who loved to talk? Does the following sound familiar? *Good morning boys and girls. Today, we are going to work on learning the capitals of the world. I think it is important to learn the capitals of the world because then we can keep up with current events. I learned the capitals of the world when I was young. In fact, we used to have contests to see who could name the most. Do you guys do that now? (No time for an answer). Well, it was pretty special. I was very good at it and could name about 40 of them without stopping ....* By this time you were probably asleep and about five minutes later, you were startled awake by the teacher who said, Sue why aren't you working? How many coaches have you had who displayed similar behaviour? Think about how much you actually learned from such a coach.

From a different perspective, think about a time you explained and demonstrated a skill and the athletes could not perform what you expected. You thought that the explanation was superb, the demonstration excellent and yet you faced blank faces after the instruction. Why did this happen?

In this chapter, we introduce some instructional techniques that, when performed effectively, can enhance athlete learning. The goal in providing various instructional techniques is to ensure the athletes understand and at the same time do not get bored from over-instruction. Often there is limited time allocated for training and every moment is precious to the athletes. They want to be involved in practising skills and tactics as much as possible, not listening to the coach telling his or her life story. This training time is the athletes' chance to improve and perhaps demonstrate that they are worthy of competing in the next competition.

> POINT TO PONDER
> I hear, I forget
> I see, I remember
> I do, I understand
> (Ancient Chinese Proverb)

Demonstrations

'A picture is worth a thousand words'. This saying is so old, yet so important when learning about sport skills. The purpose of demonstrating is to increase the athletes' understanding of skills and tactics of sports by providing an accurate model. If coaches can provide accurate pictures of what is to be practised, athletes will be able to acquire an image as a focus for the appropriate practice of sport skills and tactics. Often coaches are afraid to demonstrate a skill because they lack confidence to do so or they have not performed the skill for years. There are many ways to demonstrate an accurate skill without the coach doing it all the time.

Modelling (copying a picture) is an effective learning tool that provides an image of the skill to be performed. A model provides a guide for athletes to follow so they can practise appropriate skills. The first step in learning a skill is for the athlete to observe and comprehend the skill. One of the theories in motor learning suggests that the first phase of learning is cognitive in that athletes need to mentally process the skill to be performed.

The cognitive phase of the learning process includes five steps: Step one is where athletes observe a performance of the skill, for example in a demonstration. In step two athletes compare the model to existing skills that have been acquired from past experiences. For example, assume that some athletes can already perform a tennis serve. By understanding the skill, they may be able to cognitively compare the skills of a tennis serve to that of an overhand volleyball serve (particularly the reach at ball contact) that they are learning. This step provides mental guidance as to whether other learned skills can be used to approach a new skill. In step three athletes develop a plan of action to execute the skill. Once the mental processes of observing and comparing have occurred, the athletes should think about how to perform the skill. They may come up with a mental rehearsal process of exactly how they will initially perform. In step four the plan is put into action. This step is where the athletes actually perform the new skill. In step five the athletes receive feedback (either intrinsically, from evaluation of their own performance, or extrinsically, from the coach or other) and determine the achievement level in the skill.

Step one is an important step in gaining an appropriate understanding of the skill. If athletes skip step one and do not observe the skill, the other steps are more difficult to try. Athletes need a visual image to enhance their understanding, so demonstrations provide an important start to skill acquisition. Many coaches explain the entire skill instead, and, while some athletes may be able to create an image through an explanation of the skill, many cannot. Thus coaches should minimise verbal explanations when teaching a new skill.

Are you now convinced that demonstrations are important? Here are some guidelines for an effective demonstration for your athletes.

To Plan and Implement an Effective Demonstration

In nearly every training session coaches introduce a new skill or a part of a skill. They should plan how to teach it. In planning a demonstration, consider the following questions: Who will demonstrate? How will the skill be demonstrated? What equipment will you need to provide an effective demonstration? Where will the demonstration be given? How will I know that the athletes understood the demonstration? When should the demonstration be provided? Remember an inaccurate demonstration will not show the athletes how to perform the skill correctly.

Who

There are several options as to who can demonstrate. Take into account the difficulty of the demonstration and who is capable of performing an accurate demonstration. If you, as the coach, are going to demonstrate, remember that accurate demonstrations are essential. If you feel comfortable, demonstrate. However, you should not be afraid to admit that you cannot demonstrate a particular skill. By admitting this, athletes will be able to understand how difficult and how much time it takes to become proficient at such a skill. If coaches can admit that they are not perfect, they tend to provide an atmosphere of respect. By promoting a respectful atmosphere, athletes can understand that if they are not perfect, it is all right.

If an athlete is chosen to demonstrate, evaluate his or her individual personality and decide if he or she is capable of getting up in front of a group. Once the athlete has been selected, practise the skill with her or him to ensure a clear demonstration.

Consider also, the process of selecting athletes to demonstrate. Do you tend to pick the same high-skilled athlete to perform demonstrations? How do the other athletes feel about that person who is always in the limelight? All on the team/squad should be able to demonstrate something. Look for the contribution that each can make. If there are some who are more shy, think about using two or more athletes to demonstrate, so the quiet ones get equal limelight opportunities.

Some coaches will have access to video recorders and may be able to effectively demonstrate a skill from a videotape. Ensure that the videotape recording is shown as near to the time of the training session as possible. When using videotapes, provide verbal cues during the videotape viewing of specifically what you will work on during the training session. This will remind athletes what to focus on when they practise the skill.

Another option is to have experts come to a training session to demonstrate. The athletes will appreciate the fact that an expert took the time to come and help. Ensure this person is a good role model, one who athletes can look up to and who promotes the philosophy of 'fair play'. Athletes can be motivated to perform the skill when they see such a demonstration.

How

It is important that athletes give their full attention to and can see the demonstration. Plan the most effective formation, so that all athletes can observe the demonstration with no obstructions. For example, at a diving pool, you may only be able to line up two athletes to see the entry into the water. Arrange the others on both sides of the pool, then rotate the athletes to different points of observation to take in the skill from different perspectives.

Generally, physical education teaching literature suggests that coaches should demonstrate the whole skill first, then break the skill into parts. The first demonstration should be an actual model of the skill. For example, if a diver is learning a pike dive, the actual pike dive should be performed at normal speed. Then the coach can break down the skill into parts.

The skill should also be viewed in slow motion, so that athletes can focus on particular aspects of it. When doing this, use verbal cues to point out aspects of the skill to be practised. For example, the pike dive could be broken down on the pool deck where athletes look at the pike position. Before the pike dive is demonstrated, use verbal cues to focus on the part that you want the athletes to look at, for example, 'look at the straight knees when touching the toes'.

In order to effectively observe and cognitively process how to perform the skill, it should be viewed from different angles, such as back and front or right and left. By observing the skill at other angles, athletes may be reminded about a previously learned skill and this will enhance their understanding of the correct technique (see step two in the cognitive process to learning a skill).

Remember that if there are right- and left-handers (or footers) on the squad, show athletes the mirror image on both right and left sides. If concentrating on certain aspects of the skill, be sure to provide verbal cues so that both right and left handers can understand what to attempt.

What

What will you require to perform this demonstration accurately? What equipment will you need to be able to demonstrate the whole skill, or part of the skill? Will you need a partner, for example? Will you require goal posts, or witches hats, to be able to make certain points about the skill? Will you need modified equipment initially or can the athletes understand using regular equipment? Consider the needs of the demonstration to provide a most accurate picture to the athletes.

Where

The location of the demonstration is also an important consideration. When planning, think about the location of the sun, how many athletes you have and how many different perspectives of the skill athletes need to see, such as right vs. left, front vs. back. The location is actually just as important as the other considerations because if the athletes cannot see, they will not get an accurate picture from which to begin the learning process. One way to determine if all can see is by observing the group. Can you see all of the athletes' eyes? If not, rearrange the athletes so that you can.

Checking for Understanding

The best way to check for understanding is to get the athletes to perform the skill or part of the skill and observe what they are practising. Another effective way is to ask questions, such as 'Ramon, how would you touch your toes in the dive?' or 'Why were Angela's hands pointing that way?' If you ask the question 'Do you understand?', what do you think the response will be? They will be excited to try the new skill and will probably just say 'Yes' or nod their head in anticipation.

When

There are several stages of a training session during which demonstrations will be useful. An obvious time to have a demonstration is when athletes are learning a new skill. The demonstrations will provide feedback to athletes about their execution of the skill. Remember that athletes may be at different stages of learning, so repeating the demonstration or part of it may provide them with answers to questions that arise. This will be obvious when athletes go out to attempt the skill and one or two have difficulties. Instead of calling everyone back in to demonstrate, provide the demonstration to those who may not have understood the first time. Coaches can provide a demonstration as a reminder of skills worked on in a previous training session. Athletes often forget from week to week and a reminder demonstration is extremely effective. Another useful time to provide a demonstration is at the conclusion of a training session, as it acts as a final reminder of what they may need to practise.

The guidelines above will help to create an effective demonstration. Remember that each of the components must be planned and also that a brief demonstration is best. Try not to spend more than one minute demonstrating, then have the athletes themselves attempt the skill as soon as possible.

ACTIVITY

Using your task analysis from Chapter 4, plan a demonstration for the performance objective. When planning, ask yourself *who* will demonstrate, *what* task or subtask will be demonstrated, *when* and *where* you will provide the demonstration.

Explanation

Explanation is often an important component of a demonstration. It may also be delivered to athletes as a learning aid without an accompanying demonstration. An explanation is when the coach talks and the athletes listen. Their full attention should be gained and maintained. Explanations should be planned; they should be brief; they should contain key points. An explanation should lead directly into actual physical practice, which provides the opportunity for maximum skill development and learning.

As with demonstrating, the explanation phase of the training session is a strategy that should be planned and practised. It is important for coaches to have a space or location where all athletes meet upon a signal such as a whistle. By having such a

Instructional Techniques 107

AVOID COMPLEX, CONFUSING OR LONG-WINDED EXPLANATIONS.

routine, the time for instructions is reduced and practice time is increased. If you are planning to introduce a new skill, how will you introduce it? Will you provide the demonstration? The explanation? Or provide both? What kind of language will your athletes understand? What will the key points of your message be? On which part of the skill do you want the athletes to focus? In which part of the training session will you give this explanation? When introducing or reviewing a skill or concept, first tell the athletes why it is important to learn the concept or skill, and follow it up with an explanation and a demonstration.

Explanations and demonstrations go hand in hand as long as coaches remember not to talk during the physical demonstration. The reason for this is that athletes will have difficulty focusing on both the picture and the sound of talking. However, if coaches provide a verbal cue before the demonstration, athletes can apply the verbal cue to the picture. Remember to check for athletes' understanding of an explanation and/or demonstration.

Explanations need to be simple (matched to the developmental level of the athletes) and brief and should include reminder cues, words or phrases to help recall of the idea and to provide a picture of what is to be performed. When explaining skills or techniques, try to get athletes to focus on one concept at a time. For example, if a rowing coach wants athletes practising the stroke in the water, the coach should not then begin to discuss information about the coxswain's responsibility at the same time. Athletes should only have to focus on one skill or tactic at a time, practise it, let it become automatic, then change to another skill or tactic. Ensure your explanation complements your demonstration or vice versa.

Effective explainers:

- Make brief and clear statements during the early stages of a training session about what skills and tactics are to be learned, when to use them and how to do them.
- Provide opportunities to practise what was explained.
- Simplify or 'chunk' the information to avoid confusing the athletes with too much information.
- Direct (and redirect) attention to the important parts of the skill.
- Question athletes to determine their understanding of the explanation and remind them of previous learning.
- Question athletes to get them to make decisions and comparisons.
- Help athletes to understand by creating images and cue words that they can use to build on previous experience and skills.
- Avoid explaining during the demonstration.

'COACH, THANKS FOR NOT HAVING US LOOK INTO THE SUN, BUT HOW ABOUT SITTING AT OUR LEVEL.'

Activity

Based on the performance objective you used to plan your demonstrations, plan an explanation to provide information to your athletes about the skill. List key teaching cues (use the cue words from your task analysis) to help you remember the points to cover in the explanation.

Self-Reflection

Plan and implement a training session that focuses on the coaching strategies of demonstrating and explaining. Once again, you will need to videotape yourself coaching. While looking at the videotape, answer the following questions in reflection. Continue practising these coaching strategies until you are comfortable with your effectiveness in demonstrating and explaining.

Demonstrations and Explanations

- How did you arrange your athletes to demonstrate and explain the activity? Did you have a routine established so that athletes knew where to meet?
- Did you provide any demonstrations at the beginning of practice for a particular skill? Did you provide any demonstrations during the practice of a skill? Why or why not? List specific examples from your videotape.
- What or who provided the demonstrations? Were these effective? Provide specific examples from the videotape.
- When demonstrating did you provide the whole skill, parts of the skill or both? Provide specific examples.
- Did your athletes understand the demonstration? How did you determine whether they understood?
- Did you provide cue words with the demonstrations? Give specific examples.
- Was your explanation clear and concise?
- What kind of cue words or phrases did you use in your explanation? Did the athletes understand them?
- Did you accommodate for the different developmental levels of the athletes? Was your language clear for them?
- Were you able to offer the explanation simply and in minimal time? Why or why not?

- Did you elaborate on only one idea, or did you tend to go off on tangents?
- Was there anything you'd like to improve in your demonstrations or explanations? Explain why.

Questioning

Another component of effective coaching is the use of a high level of questioning and clarifying. Questioning can be used as a coaching strategy that will enhance learning. Coaches have traditionally used *direct instructional* techniques, such as explaining, to help athletes learn. This strategy does not involve contributions from the athletes. Basically, in using a direct approach, coaches tell the athletes what to do, how to do it and what to do to correct it. However, athletes can learn more if they are given the opportunity to work out what to do and how to do it for themselves. A questioning strategy can facilitate this. Athletes may initially be surprised at being expected to have input into solving problems and thus may not respond immediately. However, if questioning becomes part of the coaching repertoire, athletes will enjoy solving problems and will take ownership of their learning.

Solving problems through coach questioning enables athletes to explore, discover, create and generally experiment with a variety of moving and tactical processes within their specific sport. Sport and physical activity are superb ways to involve athletes in high-level thinking. Questioning will need to be tested out in each particular situation and be adapted to meet the coach's needs and athletes' expectations. Coaches are often surprised and excited by how much athletes really do know or how easily they self-learn.

Questioning has always been considered a cognitive strategy, but athletes can learn much through problem solving and questioning using movement responses. A movement response requires a physical demonstration as an answer to a question. A typical example of a question requiring a movement response is *Show us how to control the ball most effectively*, or *Show me how to grip the racquet*. Even though these phrases are not in the form of a question, the athletes must provide answers by showing the coach that they understand. Movement questions are an effective tool for enhancing physical skill learning. Athletes can identify their own or others' faults and determine correct skill technique. By actually having input through self-awareness into correcting skill performance, athletes will tend to retain the information discovered. They may determine they are incorrectly executing a skill that a coach has been trying to correct for years.

High Order and Low Order Questions

The goals of effective questioning include actively involving athletes in the learning process, enhancing task mastery and conceptual understanding and promoting both simple (low-order) and complex (high-order) thinking. When a coach wants athletes to remember specific ideas or concepts, simple or low-order questions are more appropriate. Low-order questions are often *what?* or *where?* questions, and often take place during drills. Low-order questions are factual and generally only have one possible answer. Examples of low-order questions used in coaching are:

What part of the foot do you use to kick the ball into a goal?
Where should you aim for when shooting in netball?
What is the lunge in fencing?

High-order questions require abstract or higher cognitive processes. These questions challenge athletes to apply, analyse, synthesise, evaluate and create knowledge. High-order questions are generally more appropriate for the more advanced, older athletes and enhance independent learning. More mature athletes generally have more knowledge about the subject matter and can search for multiple answers. Examples of high-order questions in the sports setting include:

How can we get the ball down the court quickly?
How can you get around the defence?
Why do we need to tuck when doing a somersault?
Why do we need to learn to change direction?

Coaches must be careful in the use of rhetorical questions. A rhetorical question is one that athletes are not expected to answer or a question that coaches answer themselves. An example of a rhetorical question is *Can you please pick up that baton?* The response *No, I can't ...* is not an option. Other examples of rhetorical questions are: *Will you please sit down?* or *What is the best way to pass to another player?*, followed by the coach answering the question him or herself. The first question directs the athletes to sit down and the second encourages the athletes to be passive.

Techniques for Effective Questioning

Questions are only as good as the answers they extract. The following are some useful tips to enhance your effective questioning skills in coaching.

Plan your Questions

To enhance the clarity and coherence of questions asked, plan the questions that will be posed during the training session. To plan appropriate questions, coaches should consider the nature of the content to be mastered and the readiness of the athletes to contribute. To practise, write down the questions you will pose for your next training session. Ensure there are a variety of high and low-order questions. It is also important to ensure that you have an answer to work towards and that you plan your questions systematically to lead to that answer. Suppose you would like the athletes to learn the footwork involved for a bowl in tenpin bowling. To determine the footwork, you would like the athletes to find out what the steps might be. Before starting to question, determine the steps up the bowling lane to where the ball is released. Then begin to create the questions. The first question might be, 'If you were to release the ball at the boundary line, what foot would have to be in the front'? Once the athletes have worked out which foot is in front where you release the ball, you might ask, 'How many steps would it take to get to the line where you release the ball?' The next question might be 'So if it takes three steps to the release line, what should your foot position be at the start?' The athletes will give many different answers, but each will work out the answer in their own way. By the end of the set of questions, a problem will have been solved, with no instruction from you.

ACTIVITY

Think of a skill in your sport that your athletes could discover themselves. Write the answer at the bottom of this activity and plan your questions to systematically arrive at the answer you have determined. The number of questions will vary, so use the outline below only as a guide.

Questions:

1. ....
2. ....
3. ....
4. ....
5. ....

Answer (skill or part of skill):

....
....

After planning the questions, read them out loud and determine whether they are clear and appropriate to the athletes' level of learning. For example, a question such as *What flight angle will be most appropriate to get the ball through the goal posts?* may not suit athletes under the age of six. Planning is the most important step, especially if you have never really used questioning as part of your coaching repertoire. Come to training prepared – know what the answers are, formulate the questions appropriately to the level of athletes, and ensure the questions are clear and coherent. After implementing the questioning strategy, coaches should evaluate the lesson (see Self-reflection on Questioning) to help improve questioning skills.

Gain Athletes' Attention

An important management strategy in conducting questioning (as in explaining and demonstrating) is to ensure that all athletes are paying attention. Establish a rule for athletes to raise their hands, and show respect for all answers. Examples of useful rules include: *When one person is talking, everyone else listens,* or *Raise your hand and wait to be called on.* Notice that both rules contain positive words and not negative words like *don't.* Once the coach has all athletes' attention, all can hear the questions, appropriate

QUESTIONING.

eye contact can be made and the coach can look for nonverbal signs of misunderstanding or excitement by the athletes. Once athletes are quiet and eager to learn, the coach can begin the planned segment using questioning strategies.

Wait Time

One of the reasons for gaining and maintaining athletes' attention is to provide wait time for athletes to formulate their responses to the question asked. Increased wait time also encourages athletes to give longer answers because they have had the opportunity to think. They will tend to volunteer more appropriate answers and failures to respond will become less frequent. The ability of athletes to respond to high-order questions is enhanced because they tend to make more speculative responses. With increased wait time, they also tend to ask more questions in return, feeling they have been given an opportunity to clarify the question. With more wait time, athletes exhibit confidence in their comments and those athletes whom coaches rate as relatively slow learners offer more questions and more responses.

Coaches should be careful not to call an athlete's name immediately after posing the question. Once the coach identifies the individual to answer the question, the others tend to relax and discontinue their thinking process.

Wait time is quite difficult when first learning how to question. Research suggests that teachers tend to answer their own questions when a wrong answer is given or that they may become impatient. Concentrate on providing appropriate wait time of 3–5 seconds. Once you have mastered wait time, coaches will find that athletes benefit more from questioning than when they are called on immediately.

Some suggestions on how to increase wait time:

- Ensure you listen to athletes' responses without repeating what athletes have said.
- Give your athletes time to think in silence while they are formulating their thoughts.
- A *yes ... but* reaction to an athlete response signals rejection of the athlete's idea.
- The athletes should provide the answers, not the coach.

Reinforcement

As athletes offer solutions, either verbally or in movement, encourage the innovative ideas that they provide – no matter how silly you perceive their answers to be. If you do not offer support for answers (both verbally and nonverbally), the athletes will be less likely to respond next time you use questioning as a coaching strategy. Put yourself in their shoes. If someone were to ask you a question in which you responded and the person commented to you *What a stupid answer*, how would you feel? Would you volunteer an answer next time? Thus, part of the process of questioning is to encourage athletes to continue to solve and try, even though they may appear to be a long way from the solution.

The difficulty here is determining whether the athlete is off task, or trying to be silly. An off-task response needs to be refocused or ignored and then reinforced on the next response attempt. Positively reinforcing appropriate behaviours will increase appropriate behaviour (see Chapter 4). Remember that different individuals respond to different types of reinforcement.

Some guidelines for effective reinforcement:

- Praise should be dependent on the athlete's answer. An example here would be *That's an interesting answer, can you tell us why you said that?*
- Praise should reinforce the athlete's response.
- Praise should be honest and sincere.
- Nonverbal reinforcement such as eye contact, thumbs up, smiling, nodding your head, clapping your hands are extremely useful forms of praise.

Probing

Probing is a strategy whereby coaches ask follow-up questions to stimulate athletes to extend, amplify or refine their answers. To probe, concentrate on providing stimulating questions to encourage athletes to expand on their thoughts. Avoid using *uh-huhs* or *okays* as these comments show a lack of interest in athletes' responses.

An example of effective probing questions:

Coach: How can we get the ball down the court?
Athlete: Dribble it.
Coach: Is there a way you can get it down faster? (probe)
Athlete: You could run faster.
Coach: That is a good answer. What other skill have we been learning to move the ball around? (probe)
Athlete: Passing.
Coach: Great. Now what is it about passing the ball that gets the ball down the court faster? (probe)
Athlete: When you pass the ball to a person, the speed of the ball is faster than when you dribble.
Coach: Now you are getting the idea. If the ball is faster when passing, what does that mean when you are being defended? (probe)
Athlete: The defender has less time to recover when you pass the ball to someone else. When you dribble, the ball is moved more slowly and therefore the defender has more time to catch up.

Probing and reinforcing promotes learning through extending current thought processes and encouraging athletes' responses.

Equity of Directing and Distributing Questions

You will notice that some athletes cannot wait to answer your questions, while others prefer to remain anonymous in the background. The athletes who volunteer readily are probably those who are most confident in their skills and their cognitive abilities. There is evidence in teaching that the students who are at the back tend to be neglected by the teacher. This will occur in the sports setting as well. As a coach, you must make a conscious effort to include all members of the team/squad in problem solving.

Allow equal time for all to contribute to the discussion. Skilful directing and distributing will provide a fair environment and one that athletes will equally contribute to if given a chance. Those who are still reluctant to participate can be encouraged by directing questions to them in a non-threatening way. If they respond to a question, they should be praised and the content of the response should be subsequently used in further discussion.

Guided Discovery of a New Skill

Another option to enhance athlete learning is to get the athletes to discover how to do the skill themselves. This method of learning is known as guided discovery. In guided discovery coaches plan a series of skill questions that help athletes progress and learn specific skills. To use guided discovery as a teaching tool, coaches need to plan the inquiry. The answer or ultimate skill should be decided and planned first, then the skill questions arranged for the athletes to discover the answer. Demonstrations of the skills and parts of skills are then provided by athletes as they discover the solution to the problem. An illustration of discovering how to find the open space after a dribble in soccer, might better explain what is meant:

Coach: 'Everyone get a partner, one ball between two. Pass to your partner in any way you like.'
Athletes: Passing all kinds of different ways.
Coach: 'Now pass to your partner as she runs forward.'
Athletes: Passing to partners and aiming everywhere. Some athletes are having to turn around and run for the ball, some are going forward nicely.
Coach: 'Now, if you want to make sure that your partner goes forward (towards the goal), where do you want the pass to go?'
Johnny: 'They should go behind the person'.
Coach: 'Okay, let's see how that works Debbie. All go out with your partners and try to pass behind the person.' *After the athletes have tried this, the coach asks:* 'Did that work?'
Athletes: (in unison) 'NO!!'
Coach: 'Why didn't it work?'
Athletes: 'Because we had to keep coming backwards.'
Coach: 'Okay, so how shall we do it this time?'
Kirsten: 'We should pass it to the front of the player.'
Coach: 'Okay, let's try what Kirsten said.'

From this step the coach might get the athletes to practise running forward. After they have mastered the concept, the coach might call them in again and try the same sort of discovery for passing and running to a space. An example might include, 'Okay, now that we can pass it well, what do you think the player that just passed the ball should do?'.

Notice that the coach did not provide an explanation or demonstration, but the athletes figured out the way to pass forward by themselves. Any method where athletes have to figure out how a skill is performed will not only enhance the retention and understanding of that skill, but athletes will get more practice opportunities and will take control of their own skill experience. Using a method like this, athletes tend to remember more because they are doing it, rather than watching a coach explain and demonstrate.

SELF-REFLECTION

Plan and implement a training session that includes the coaching strategy of questioning. After practising the questioning strategy, videotape a training session. Observe and analyse your use of questions from the videotape. Answer the following questions with regard to your questioning technique. Continue this practice or process until you are comfortable with using questioning skills.

Enjoy your questioning session, it will be very rewarding. Do not give up if the session does not work the first time; your athletes may not be accustomed to answering questions. The use of effective questioning will further enhance the coaching process and promote athlete learning.

- How clear and coherent were the questions that you asked your athletes?
- When asking questions, did you have all the athletes' attention?
- Was your pause or wait time long enough (3–5 seconds)? Compare the answers from the athletes when you did and did not wait.
- Did all the athletes have a chance to answer the questions? Why or why not?
- Did you listen and accept athlete responses?
- What reinforcement strategies did you use for athletes' responses? Were they effective? Why or why not?
- After listening to the answers, were you able to probe to extend the athletes understanding? List examples of your probing questions and analyse them.
- List the questions that you asked during the session. How many were high-order questions and how many were low-order questions? Was the ratio effective? Why or why not?

Now that you have used questioning, how did it go? Were the athletes quite willing to solve the problems you posed? What were the athletes' reactions to becoming part of this session?

Summary

1. Effective instructional strategies are essential to enhance athlete learning.
2. The cognitive phase of athlete learning involves five steps: (1) observing a skill performance (demonstration), (2) comparing the model to an existing skill performance, (3) developing a plan of action to perform the skill, (4) putting the plan into action and (5) receiving feedback from internal and/or external sources.
3. An effective demonstration is an instructional strategy that provides athletes with a model to follow.
4. To plan an effective demonstration, consider who will demonstrate and what, how and where the skill will be demonstrated.
5. An explanation is an instructional strategy that is used directly by the coach to introduce, provide or expand on information to be learned. An explanation often accompanies a demonstration.
6. Coaches should check for athletes' understanding of a demonstration and/or explanation by asking specific questions about the information given.
7. Questioning is an instructional strategy that enhances athletes' learning by putting the learning into their hands.
8. Questioning in sport includes the use of movement responses that enables athletes to answer questions by physically demonstrating the answers.
9. High-order questions challenge athletes to apply, analyse, synthesis, evaluate or create knowledge. High-order questions have multiple answers.
10. Low-order questions require athletes to remember specific ideas or concepts. Low-order questions generally have a specific answer.

11. Effective questioning requires: planning the questions, ensuring you have athletes' attention during questioning, providing 3–5 seconds wait time after posing a question, probing to try to expand on or redirect answers and distributing questions equally amongst everyone.
12. Guided discovery is a questioning strategy to guide athletes to answers. In guided discovery, the coach never gives answers, the athletes discover them.

Further Reading

Coaching Association of Canada (1988), *Coaching Theory, Level 1: National Coaching Certification Programme,* Gloucester, Ontario: Coaching Association of Canada.

Fitts, P.M. and Posner, M.I. (1976), *Human Performance,* Belmont, CA: Brooks/Cole.

Graham, G. (1992), *Teaching Physical Education: Becoming a Master Teacher,* Champaign, IL: Human Kinetics.

Mosston, M. (1972), *Teaching: From Command to Discovery,* Belmont, CA: Wadsworth.

Randall, L. (1992), *Systematic Supervision for Physical Education,* Champaign, IL: Human Kinetics.

Sadker, M. and Sadker, D. (1986), *Classroom Teaching Skills,* D. Heath and Co.

Siedentop, D. (1991), *Developing Teaching Skills in Physical Education,* Mountain View, CA: Mayfield.

Chapter 7

Enhancing Skill Technique

- Observing and Analysing
- Effective Feedback

Some of the challenges faced when observing and analysing are how to observe the skill, knowing what to look for and finding the best ways to help athletes enhance skill technique. There is much to observe and analyse and many environmental factors may influence athletes' performance. Often instant decisions must be made as to how to change the skill or how to make the drill easier so that the athletes can learn more efficiently. To be effective observers and analysers of skill technique, coaches must determine the factors that affect performance, including the mood of the athlete, the weather, the state of the facilities and equipment, then make judgements and provide sound advice (feedback). Coaches must know the developmental levels of each individual athlete to make a decision on how difficult or easy to make the skill. In this chapter, we offer some practical tips for coaches to successfully observe and analyse athletes' skill technique performance. After developing observation and analysis strategies, coaches have to be able to communicate the information to athletes through positive and effective feedback. The purpose of feedback, and guidelines on how to develop effective feedback strategies, are outlined in this chapter.

Observing and Analysing

Observing and analysing skill technique can be done with the entire team/squad or with an individual athlete performing a skill. When observing and analysing the team or squad, coaches are partly concerned with such questions as 'Did the athletes understand my explanation and demonstration?' or 'Were the drills at an appropriate level of difficulty?' There is some information about these questions in Chapter 6 on 'Instruction'. This chapter focuses on observing and analysing individual athletes, so that coaches can help enhance athletes' personal skill technique performance.

An effective observer and analyser is able to focus on a small number of parts of the skill technique that are important. One of the first considerations is to determine how athletes *should* perform the skill technique. To enhance your observing and analysing strategies, identify parts of the skill technique and decide what is important, why it is important and where improvement can be made (see task analysis in Chapter 4). A task analysis needs to be created for every skill technique in your sport. For example, if a coach is planning to teach a drop kick in rugby, he or she should list, in the task analysis, all the parts of the skill technique and coaching cues for it. The task analysis of a skill technique provides information to enhance the coach's decision-making process about what to correct or praise about athletes' performance of skill technique. The task analysis should identify the purpose of the skill and break the skill into parts (subtasks). Once the task analysis is completed, an *observation plan* should be designed so that coaches can observe and analyse the strengths, weaknesses and errors of the actual performance of the skill technique. The observation plan is a blueprint of how, when and where you will observe and analyse skill techniques during a training session.

> **POINT TO REMEMBER**
> You should develop a task analysis for every skill technique in your sport. Once it is developed, your observation and analysis strategies will be more efficient.

The observation stage is important because coaches should now plan when, how, where and what to observe to make an effective analysis of the skill technique. If you attempt to watch the entire skill technique, there may be confusion about what aspect needs the most work. Therefore, when trying to refine an athlete's skill technique, ensure the observation plan focuses on one part at a time. The task analysis design should identify each part of the skill technique. Remember that the arms and legs will probably move faster than other parts of the body, so look at the slower moving parts, then try to focus on the faster moving parts. It helps to observe the entire skill technique for a substantial period of time before attempting to analyse it. Also, when first learning a skill technique, athletes often perform it in several different ways while they cognitively process the movement (see Chapter 6).

Other decisions coaches should make when designing the observation plan are:

1. Questions: How are you going to observe or look at the athletes' skill technique? Will you view them during their actual performance or will you use video to record the skill technique?
   Reflection: Video is a powerful tool for coaches and athletes to observe and analyse performance. Using video, coaches can view the skill technique in slow motion, view it as many times as needed and assess every part of it. Another benefit of video analysis is that athletes can sit and view their skill technique with their coach and they can analyse it together.
2. Question: On which parts of the skill technique will you focus?
   Reflection: Using the task analysis, select the content on which to focus so that an observation plan can be designed. Observe the athletes for as many times as needed to gain enough information to make an accurate analysis. Are there any safety

aspects to consider when observing? For example, you may need to spot while observing, or ensure that you are being protected from being hit with the bat or the ball.
3. Question: Where will you position yourself to see the skill technique?
   Reflection: When athletes are first learning a skill technique, coaches should try to position themselves so they can see the greatest amount of movement. After making an initial observation, try to move around to gain several different vantage points to enhance the analysis. The observation position depends on the skill technique being performed, but ensure that you are in an appropriate place to see various phases of the skill technique. Coaches are notorious for standing in one place to observe.

OBSERVATION POSITIONS SHOULD BE CAREFULLY SELECTED.

4. Question: When will you observe the skill technique?
   Reflection: At the beginning of training sessions athletes are generally fresher and therefore may process the skill technique better at this stage of the training session. In determining when to observe, also consider how warmed up the athletes are. Coaches should perhaps observe the skill technique before the athletes are too tired to execute it effectively or they may decide that the athletes need several attempts before observing the performance. These decisions should be made when creating the observation plan.

Once the observation plan is made, it will be easier to actually observe the athletes. When observing, you should carry out the observation plan that has been set. To make this step easier, you will have to be completely familiar with the skill technique that is being performed. Refer back to the task analysis for a breakdown of various parts of the skill technique that will be observed and analysed. Below is an example of an observation plan that is based on the task analysis presented in Chapter 4.

Observation Plan

Content	Task Analysis	How	What	Where	When
Lay-up	dribble	observe 3X during training	control of the ball	front on, to see push of the ball	middle of training
	run-up	observe 2 X	steps to run-up	from side, then back	as with dribble
	take off	watch video 1X	the hurdle	from side	after training with athletes
	shot	watch video 1X	the follow-through	from side and front	after training with athletes
	landing	observe in training 2X	bent knees	from behind	middle of training

ACTIVITY

Using the observation plan below, plan one or two skill techniques that you will observe and analyse during your next training session. Use your task analysis from Chapter 4 to help you create the observation plan.

Observation Plan

Content	Task Analysis	How	What	Where	When

Just as athletes must practise their skills, coaches should practise their observing and analysing strategies. Past coaching experience will have increased the effectiveness of observation and analysis strategies. Trial and error plays a major role in determining what works best for each athlete. However, by designing a task analysis, coaches will be able to enhance their coaching strategies and provide athletes with insights and knowledge to effectively develop skill techniques. Once you have developed a task analysis and observation plan for each skill technique in your sport, this information will be readily available every time the skill technique is taught. Use the knowledge to detect and correct errors and thereby help participants improve their skill technique.

SELF-REFLECTION

Design (or use the one you created from the previous activities) a task analysis and observation plan for a skill technique in your sport. Videotape an athlete performing the skill. While the athlete is being videotaped, perform an observation analysis using your task analysis and observation plans. Determine if the video analysis is more effective than making the observation and analysis during your training session. Is what you observe and analyse in the live setting the same as what you observe and analyse watching the videotape of the athlete?

After you have observed and analysed the specific skill technique, based on your designed task analyses and observation plans, videotape yourself coaching. Use self-reflection about your application of observing and analysing strategies. The following reflective questions may help you:

- Were you able to observe and analyse one part of the skill technique at a time? Explain some of your experiences.
- Were you able to keep all athletes within sight during the training session? Why or why not? If not, how did you accommodate those athletes who were not within your sight?
- Did you scan your athletes frequently to look for errors or correct skills?
- Did you distribute your observation attention equally? Why or why not?
- Did you respond positively to appropriate skill movement or just correct skill errors?
- Did you gain an appropriate vantage point of the skill to enable an effective analysis?

Effective Feedback

One way to correct or maintain performance is through feedback. Feedback is defined as the information that is available during or after a performance of skill technique. It is provided to enhance athletes' learning. Without feedback, athletes may not know how they are performing, so their skill technique may not change. Athletes who are provided feedback tend to acquire greater quality skill technique.

Feedback fulfils two main functions: informational and motivational. Informational feedback provides athletes with verbal comments or nonverbal gestures about how the skill technique was performed. Motivational feedback provides athletes with verbal or non-verbal cues to encourage or discourage the continuous attempt of the skill technique. Although the two functions can take on one role, they can also be an outcome of each other. In other words, informational feedback can be motivational in and of itself. A tone of voice or a nonverbal gesture combined with information of the performance can still be motivating or demotivating.

There are two types of feedback: *intrinsic* and *extrinsic*. Intrinsic feedback is feedback that athletes receive as a natural consequence of their performance of skill technique. It comes in the form of kinaesthetic, tactile, visual and auditory sensory systems, for example such things as the feel of the ball, or the sound of the ball hitting the racquet, or the sight of the the ball going through the net. Intrinsic feedback provides athletes with knowledge about special characteristics of their sport and determines positive and negative performance of skill technique. Extrinsic feedback is that which is given from an external source such as the coach, other athletes, parents and spectators. It can be verbal or nonverbal and can help or detract athletes from improving their skill techniques. Extrinsic feedback can supplement intrinsic feedback.

Intrinsic Feedback

Intrinsic feedback is important. It comes from athletes using their senses to determine how they have executed a skill technique. Athletes can determine a good catch or pass, for example, the sound of the ball hitting the fingertips, or the sound of the ball entering the right place in the glove. In squash a good hit can be determined by the sound of the ball hitting the strings. In canoeing, an athlete knows what the sound of the paddle entering the water should be. Athletes can also feel how muscles are reacting while performing different movements. When athletes comment that 'it felt good!' they are reflecting positive intrinsic feedback. Athletes can also tell a successful or unsuccessful performance of skill technique through the sense of touch. In diving, for instance, athletes can evaluate their dive according to how they enter the water. Coaches can, however, play a role in enhancing intrinsic feedback by asking their athletes how the skill technique felt, or sounded. Athletes can see how well they performed using mirrors or videos to watch themselves. Intrinsic feedback develops an athlete's self-awareness and ability to determine how well they performed a particular skill technique.

The Query Theory

We often forget that athletes can determine their own errors and strengths in their performance of skill technique and it is important to give them more opportunities to be able to judge their own performance of skill technique. You may recall some of the surprises and elation when upon seeing themselves on videotape athletes could finally understand what you had been telling them. A coaching strategy to give athletes more of an opportunity to analyse their skills has been suggested by David Hadfield (1994) and is known as the Query Theory.

Basically, the Query Theory recommends that coaches encourage improvement in skill techniques through athlete self-awareness. This self-awareness is gained by providing ways for athletes to solve problems about the performance of skill technique by themselves, rather than telling them what to do and how to correct the skill. For example, if you are trying to get an athlete to determine the correct pass to make in netball, give them a situation and get them to tell you the correct answer. In Chapter 6 we touched on guided discovery. The Query Theory reiterates guided discovery and problem solving as a learning process. The purpose of using self-awareness as athlete feedback is that until the athlete can kinaesthetically understand what the movement feels like, they cannot make the necessary adjustments. If the athlete cannot feel it or understand it, the athlete cannot change it. A cricket example is presented from David Hadfield's (1994) Query Theory.

> I was coaching a group of youngsters in a net and was trying to help one lad rid himself of a very common technical error – moving the back foot towards the leg side (i.e. backwards) just as the bowler was delivering the ball. ... Many coaches of young cricketers have spent a considerable amount of time trying to correct the fault. I was following my normal routine of identifying the fault ('you're moving your back foot to leg as the bowler bowls, Ned'), explaining why it wasn't a good idea and suggesting a correction ('Keep your feet still, with the weight on the balls of your feet, until the ball is released, Ned'). As usual, it seemed the lad had great difficulty in changing what he was doing. Seeing a demolition brick lying at the foot of the nearby clubrooms, I had a stroke of inspiration. I got the brick and placed it behind the young batsman's back heel – the one that was causing the problems with backwards movement. I then instructed him to bat as normal. The bowler ran in and let the ball go and as usual, the young batsman went to shift his foot backwards. This time however, his heel ran into the unyielding mass of the brick and came to a rapid halt. The lad was so surprised that he didn't even attempt to hit the ball and turning to me with a look of astonishment and amusement on his face, said something like 'Crickey you're right Dave! I am moving my back foot aren't I?' At the end of the session, he had stopped moving his back foot (p. 16–17).

The cricket example above demonstrates a method that allows athletes to work out problems by themselves, with a bit of assistance from the coach, such as a brick as in this instance, or even a question or two. Self-awareness is a key to improving athletes' skill techniques.

THE QUERY THEORY.

ACTIVITY

List a common error in your sport in the table below. Evaluate that error and design a way for athletes to learn on their own about it. Ask yourself what athletes could do to learn to perform the skill technique correctly without having any input from you. An example is provided based on the cricket story above.

Common Error	Query Theory Approach	Your Feedback
Stepping backwards when batting	Put brick behind foot of batter	Keep your feet still with the weight on the balls of your feet, until the ball is released. You're moving your foot back as the bowler bowls.

Your turn:

Common Error	Query Theory Approach	Your Feedback

Extrinsic Feedback

Providing appropriate and timely feedback to athletes is a strategy that coaches should practise and review. Athletes should to be able to understand the feedback and from it modify the movement. In Chapter 4 we talked about coaching cues. To ensure feedback is understood, use coaching cues to help remind athletes about parts of the skill technique to perform. After giving the coaching cues, observe subsequent performances to determine if the feedback was understood. Give additional feedback if needed, then progress to the next athlete.

The degree of precision (general or specific) is important for providing effective feedback. There are times when providing general feedback is useful, but it is more important to provide the athlete with specific information about how to improve, or what was correct. General feedback such as 'Good', 'Well done' and 'Good on ya mate' provide sources of positive feedback that nurture the caring environment, but does not specify what was good, or why it was well done.

Specific feedback contains information that tells athletes what they need to know to improve or continue to perform. Athletes benefit from obtaining specific information from coaches or others about the skill technique. Some examples of specific feedback are:

> Your bowl is accurate, but your arm should follow through afterwards to get more power.
> That was much better because your chin was tucked into your chest. See if you can tuck your knees into your chest a bit more.
> Wow. You have really improved your batting grip. By holding the bat with the right hand on top, you will find more stability.
> The balance in the landing was superb because you were able to bend your knees and were ready to make the pass.

Coaches should provide young children and low-skilled performers with feedback that relates to gross aspects of movement patterns. For example, in tennis the children need feedback about their swings rather than about how to aim the ball. Once the athlete has matured or become more skilled, coaches should provide more complex feedback because the athletes can process more precise information.

The *nature* (positive, neutral or negative) of feedback is an important element in the provision of effective feedback. *Positive* feedback provides encouragement to athletes and may enhance the self-esteem of an athlete. Everybody likes to receive praise, especially if it is sincere and honest. *Negative* feedback does not encourage or motivate athletes to perform, and sarcasm from a coach is counterproductive to athlete motivation and may cause them to give up easily. Coaches are notorious for recognising and correcting errors more often than noticing correct aspects of the movement. One of the most commonly used forms of negative feedback is the word 'Don't'. If you said to an athlete 'Don't think about how hard the ball is', you may have created fear for the athlete. What do you think of when someone says 'Don't worry'? Negative feedback can hinder athletes' learning. Be cautious in how and when you use negative feedback. *Neutral* feedback has no positive or negative connotations. It usually provides more of a prompt, such as 'Remember to use one hand for balance'. Coaches often use neutral feedback when athletes are first learning skills, to remind athletes of important points of the skill technique.

Immediate feedback is more useful than delayed feedback because it provides the athlete with information just after the skill performance. Often coaches remind athletes of ways to perform skill techniques several minutes after the skill was performed. Athletes cannot remember or feel exactly how they performed if the feedback is too delayed.

Whether the feedback is *congruent* or *incongruent* is also important. Congruent feedback focuses on the coaching cue verbalised or demonstrated to the team/squad. Congruent feedback corresponds to the idea just presented to athletes. The feedback provided should relate specifically to what athletes are practising. If a rugby league player is working on the follow-through of a lateral pass, it is important to focus only on the follow-through of the lateral pass. Feedback on other aspects of the lateral pass is incongruent feedback and would distract the athlete from focusing on the original goal – the follow-through. Incongruent feedback may load athletes with too much information. By planning the skill technique and the specific skill performance, coaches can focus on one or two aspects of the skill at one time.

Now that you have considered effective feedback techniques, feedback needs to be formulated and given. Sport psychologists favour the sandwich approach (see Chapter 5). An example of the sandwich approach:

> Scenario: The coach sees that Simon's foot position is making it difficult for him to hit the target.
> Coach: Simon, you are bending your knees enough, but if you point your toes towards the target, you will come much closer to where you are aiming to bowl.

POINT TO PONDER
> When I first began to realise that I was unequally distributing feedback was when one of my hockey players (a 12-year-old) asked why I always talked to those who could not perform the skill well. I hadn't realised that I wasn't giving positive feedback and further encouragement to those who were doing well. I always felt that the players who needed to develop their skills were the ones who needed the most feedback. I was wrong. The higher skilled players need as much feedback as the lower skilled players or they won't continue to develop.

Guidelines for providing extrinsic coach feedback:

- Frequent feedback is desirable for skill learning and improved performance. Insincere feedback is not desirable.
- Feedback should be sufficiently precise to identify relevant aspects of the skill performance, but not so detailed as to confuse the learner. Feedback should be given according to the developmental level of the athletes. If they are unskilled or young, coaches should provide more information about general and gross aspects of the skill.
- Feedback should be followed by opportunities to practise the skill and implement the prescription.
- Coaches should try to be consistent when providing feedback for both high and low-skilled athletes.

SELF-REFLECTION

As mentioned several times in this book already, every athlete should be given equal attention. It is known that often teachers favour one group of children. Some favour the brightest, some favour the most attractive. Similarly some coaches favour higher-skilled, some lower-skilled athletes. Some coaches may provide more feedback to boys, some to girls. Ensure that you are providing equal feedback to your athletes. From one of your coaching videotapes, analyse the feedback you provide for your athletes using the following reflective questions:

- Which (if any) athletes did not receive feedback from you? (To determine this, write down all the athletes' names on a piece of paper and tick their name when you provide them with feedback, then designate whether the feedback was +, – or 0).
- Did you tend to favour any particular group for example, the highly skilled or the more personable athletes?
- Did you tend to use specific or general feedback? Give some examples from your videotape.
- Was your feedback congruent with your verbal coaching cues? Give examples.
- Are you satisfied with the ratio of positive to neutral to negative feedback? What was the ratio?
- Did you vary your positive terms? Or did 'good' or 'well done' predominate? Give examples.
- Was the feedback you provided sincere? Why or why not?
- Was your feedback given immediately? Give some examples.
- How did the athletes respond to your positive feedback?
- Did you ask the athletes to determine their own errors? How did this work?

POINT TO PONDER
I watched a coach turn into a different person after viewing himself giving feedback. He commented 'I always bark at the kids. I'm so negative'. To change, he began getting the athletes more involved in the learning process by questioning them about how the skill felt. The athletes were surprised at first, but then really started enjoying the sessions because they were helping themselves learn.

Summary

1. To provide athletes with information about their skill technique, coaches should develop effective observing and analysing strategies.
2. A task analysis is a valuable tool to help coaches create an observation plan. A task analysis and observation plan should be created for every skill technique in your sport.
3. An observation plan includes what, when, how and where coaches will observe athletes. An observation plan enhances coaches' ability to analyse skill technique because it identifies important sub-tasks to observe and analyse.
4. Feedback serves an informational and motivational purpose and provides athletes with information and reinforcement to correct and/or maintain skill technique performance.

5. Intrinsic feedback comes from athletes themselves and is a natural consequence of skill technique performance. Extrinsic feedback is obtained from external sources such as the coach.
6. The Query Theory is a self-awareness strategy whereby athletes discover their own strengths and weaknesses of skill technique performance.
7. General feedback provides athletes with no specific information or direction of focus. Specific feedback provides athletes with specific information about their skill technique performance.
8. Feedback is classified as positive, negative or neutral. Coaches generally give too much negative feedback.
9. Feedback should be given immediately after the performance of skill technique, rather than delayed.
10. Congruent feedback focuses on the specific task that athletes are practising.

Further Reading

Canadian Association of Coaching (1988), *National Coaching Certification Program,* Canada: Coaching Association of Canada.
Chistina, R.W. and Corcos, D.M. (1988), *Coaches' Guide to Teaching Sport Skills,* Champaign, IL: Human Kinetics.
Gallway, W.T. (1974), *The Inner Game of Tennis,* Auckland, New Zealand: Bantom.
Graham, G. (1992), *Teaching Children Physical Education,* Champaign, IL: Human Kinetics.
Hadfield, D. (1994), 'The Query Theory', *New Zealand Coach,* vol. 3, no. 4, pp. 16–20.
Martens, R. (1990), *Successful Coaching,* Champaign, IL: Human Kinetics.
Williams, J.M. (1993), *Applied Sport Psychology,* Mountain View, CA: Mayfield.

Chapter 8

Enhancing Performance with Mental Skills

- What are Mental Skills?
- How to Include Mental Skills Training with Physical Training

One of the primary roles of coaches is to help athletes improve their performance. When improvement occurs athletes tend to find participation enjoyable. Improved performance can also lead to increased self-esteem, motivation, confidence and belief in the training programme (including belief in the coach). Performance enhancement, however, is not just improving a personal best or an individual's top level of performance. A large part of performance enhancement is increasing the consistency of performance. Instead of having the quality of performance fluctuate, with high peaks but low troughs, athletes should be able to maintain a consistently high level of performance. Many aspects of performance enhancement relate to physical techniques and tactics that are specific for each sport, or even particular positions or events within the sport. Coaches should check sport specific sources for these contributions to performance. Physical fitness will also contribute to performance, but it is not the purpose of this book to explain exercise physiology. This chapter instead focuses on how mental skills can help both you and your athletes achieve better and more consistent performances.

What are Mental Skills?

Few (if any) immature athletes dependably produce the same quality of performance time after time. Various factors can affect performance consistency. For instance, when training programmes are designed to have athletes peak at a particular point in time, there will be physiological factors that keep athletes from achieving their best during other phases of training. Many athletes also will have sub-par performances where there is illness or injury. But even taking these more obvious considerations into account, there are still many athletes (and coaches) who do not consistently perform at the level they are capable of achieving. So why are people inconsistent in their performances? The following activity should help you answer this question.

ACTIVITY

For each of the situations in the following list, note whether you believe it is 'A' something that contributes to the inconsistent performance of your athletes and/or 'C' something that contributes to your own inconsistent performance as coach. (Remember to use pencil or photocopy activities.)

- ___ thinking about work or study
- ___ being distracted by someone in the stands
- ___ worrying about winning (thinking about the outcome)
- ___ being uncertain about own abilities (self-doubt)
- ___ worrying about the performance of team mates
- ___ being indecisive (changing your mind half way through an action)
- ___ struggling with a new technique early on in a competition
- ___ having no plan
- ___ being too anxious
- ___ feeling too much pressure from others
- ___ thinking you have won
- ___ thinking the competition is a lost cause
- ___ thinking about the next round of competition (while still involved in the current round)
- ___ worrying about what others might think
- ___ being concerned about other people's performances
- ___ thinking about what someone said or did to you before competition
- ___ skipping the normal pre-competition routine
- ___ feeling like being somewhere else (mind wanders)
- ___ feeling burnt out
- ___ having unrealistic expectations
- ___ dwelling on mistakes
- ___ having doubts about physical preparation or equipment
- ___ falling in love
- ___ trying too hard
- ___ participating in a competition below your ability level
- ___ participating in a competition above your ability level
- ___ spacing out (visiting another planet)
- ___ thinking about a previous injury
- ___ being self-conscious performing in front of others
- ___ disagreeing with officials
- ___ losing your temper
- ___ thinking about what it is you do not want to do

___ being distracted by the opposition
___ thinking about the weather, venue
___ having no reason for being there
___ realising the competition is running late
___ doing unexpectedly well
___ doing unexpectedly poorly
___ being bored between events/games
___ thinking about what impact the outcome of the competition might have
___ swearing at yourself
___ having to reach preset criteria/having to qualify
___ performing in front of selectors
___ having ongoing arguments with others
___ (add your own) _____
___ _____

Assuming at least some of the situations listed in the above activity contribute, at times, to inconsistent or poor performances for either yourself or your athletes, the good news is that developing mental skills can help. The second section of this chapter will provide examples of strategies that can be used to help control or cope with some of these situations.

Athletes generally state that between 40 per cent and 90 per cent of their performance is dependent on psychological factors. Although most athletes agree that mental skills account for at least 50 per cent of performance, much less than 50 per cent of training time is spent on developing specific mental skills. Although we are not suggesting that you spend half of your training time on the development of mental skills, we do recommend that mental skills be incorporated into training programmes.

Mental skills are ignored by coaches and athletes for three reasons: (1) individuals do not know how to develop mental skills; (2) individuals believe that people have either the mental skills or they do not; and (3) individuals feel there is something wrong with them if they try to work on mental skills. They feel that admitting that their mental skills can be improved is confessing that they are mentally ill.

Mental skills help athletes and coaches perform to the best of their current level of ability, help people enjoy their participation in sport more and can actually help athletes and coaches develop skills for use in situations other than sport. Mental skills are not designed as a treatment for individuals with clinical psychological problems.

Mental skills influence performance and just like physical skills, they can be improved through practice. Mental skills do not take the place of physical skills and physical fitness, but they do contribute to the overall sporting experience. Just as there are numerous physical skills, there are also diverse mental skills. Some examples of mental skills that can be successfully included in sporting programmes follow.

Concentration and Attention

During training and competition both athletes and coaches should be focused on what is currently happening. Performance will not be optimal if individuals are thinking about what they are going to have for dinner when they get home from training or thinking about who is in the crowd during competitions. Developing concentration and attention skills helps people focus on important cues and ignore irrelevant information or distractions. A discussion of different attentional styles was presented in Chapter 3.

Optimal Arousal

Arousal level, or activation level, affects individuals' ability to calm down when they are feeling uptight, and pick themselves up when they are feeling flat. Performance can be less than optimal if arousal levels are too high or too low. Under-arousal most frequently occurs during training sessions or when participating in a competition below one's ability level. Over-arousal usually occurs when feeling anxious, pressured or stressed. Over-arousal in sport can result in 'choking' – performance just seems to disintegrate. Coaches are not immune to over-arousal. Coaches can make poor decisions when anxious, pressured or stressed.

There is no single optimal level of arousal. The optimal level of arousal will vary with sports, positions and individuals. Generally, a higher level of arousal would be expected for someone weightlifting than for someone putting in golf. In rugby, kicking a goal would generally require a lower level of arousal than would packing a scrum. Within a specific sport, position or event, however, there will be individual differences. Some people perform their best when feeling laid back, relaxed and calm. Others need to be highly activated to perform their best and some even need to feel angry. An analogy can be made with the expression, 'having butterflies in your stomach'. For some people the optimal level of arousal involves having no butterflies whatsoever. Others may like a few butterflies flitting around. Some people may feel optimally aroused when they have butterflies in their stomach, but are flying in formation; in other words, the individual has the butterflies under control. A few may even prefer having bats to butterflies! Whatever the desired state, individuals can learn to use mental skills to achieve their own optimal level of arousal.

ACTIVITY

On a scale of 1 to 10, with '1' being sluggish as if you had just woken up and '10' being the most activated you have ever been in your life (with the adrenalin really pumping), estimate where on the scale you need to be to perform your best in the following situations:

Score Situation
___ threading a needle
___ running to catch a bus or train
___ throwing a ball as far as you can
___ being interviewed for a job or a promotion
___ explaining to an official why you disagree with a call or ruling
___ walking across a balance beam.

If you compared your scores to somebody else's you would probably discover some more differences.

Imagery

Imagery, sometimes called visualisation, is the ability of a person to mentally recreate objects, persons, skills, movements and situations, while not actually being involved with these. Although there is not complete agreement on how imagery works, it is generally accepted that imagery provides a mental and physical blueprint of the performance. Basically, our minds cannot distinguish between a vivid image and the real thing. It is likely that the more you do something, the easier it is to do. Using imagery, you may perform a skill correctly many times, so that when you have to physically perform the skill, your mind thinks, 'Well, I've been there and done that, so this should be pretty easy'.

Imagery is valuable because it is not physically fatiguing. Some individuals want to have an instant experience of having perfectly performed a particular skill immediately prior to competition. A certain percentage of these people can actually physically tire themselves before competition by performing the physical skill over and over. Imagery is a more effective alternative.

An injured athlete can maintain his or her technique by mentally rehearsing the skill (although unfortunately imagery cannot maintain fitness). Imagery can be practised anywhere, anytime, such as while sitting on a bus on the way to competition or while washing your hair. The organisation and co-ordination of movement take place in the brain. The learning process is accelerated by using imagery because when we image a movement, the requisite organisation and co-ordination are still taking place.

IMAGERY.

Imagery can be used to help us set goals, control emotions, develop confidence, improve concentration, practise physical skills mentally and even heal injuries and control pain. There are two aspects of imagery, however, that must be developed for it to be effective: vividness and control. The more vivid an image is, the more likely our brains are going to think the image is the real thing. A silent, unfocused black and white image will not be as effective as an image using technicolour and surround sound. When we are involved in sporting situations, we are not just seeing things. All of our senses are involved. Therefore, when imaging, all the senses should be incorporated.

A vivid image by itself will not necessarily be effective. Images also need to be controlled. For example, Steve was a basketball player who could easily make free throws during training, but could not make a free throw to save his life during the pressure of competition. Steve had very vivid imagery so he decided to image himself making free throws when the pressure was on. Although this strategy of using imagery was good in theory, in practice it did not work because Steve had no control over his imagery. In his images when he dribbled the ball before shooting, the ball would stick to the floor, never even giving him a chance to shoot. Obviously this lack of control only increased his anxiety when it came to shooting free throws in competition. Therefore, when using imagery with your athletes, it is important to help them develop vividness and control before expecting imagery to be a helpful tool.

Self-confidence and Self-talk

Self-confidence is the realistic expectation individuals have about being successful, or the general faith in their ability to perform. A person must, of course, be physically capable of performing the skills required (in other words, confidence alone will not mean you will be able to perform). Confidence is especially important in situations where adverse consequences are expected from a poor performance, for example when competing in selection trials or elimination tournaments.

The relationship between self-confidence and performance can be considered as a circular or spiral one, each component influencing the other. If you have a slightly off performance, you may begin to doubt yourself, which will contribute to another poor performance, and so on. This downward spiral can be broken by either improving performance or improving self-confidence.

Confidence is related to anxiety as well as to performance. Anxiety and self-confidence have an inverse relationship. In other words, as confidence increases, anxiety decreases. Similarly, as anxiety increases, confidence decreases. Techniques that help decrease anxiety can also serve to increase confidence.

Negative self-talk often enters the picture when self-confidence is taking a bit of a dive. Negative self-talk impairs performance and creates stress. Usually when we are having bad performances and feeling stressed, we are not enjoying ourselves very much. Realistic and constructive positive self-talk, on the other hand, can help us focus our attention and increase our confidence. Once we learn to control that little voice in our heads, we begin to control our self-confidence.

POINT TO PONDER
Nobody can make you feel inferior without your consent.
(Eleanor Roosevelt)

Additional Mental Skills

Motivation can be developed and enhanced. Goal setting is the most useful skill to help the maintenance and enhancement of motivation (see Chapter 5).

Mental processes can also be developed to improve organisational and control skills in such areas as communication (Chapter 5), time management (Chapter 10), team building (Chapter 3), overcoming jet lag, dealing with the media and psychological rehabilitation from injury. See the reference list at the end of this chapter for additional sources of information about mental skills.

How to Include Mental Skills Training with Physical Training

The main objective of mental skills development is to help individuals control the controllable. Goals help control motivation levels. Relaxation and stress management skills help control arousal levels. Controlling self-talk helps develop self-confidence and also attentional focus. Imagery helps individuals control physical skills and emotions. Appropriate forms of concentration help control attention.

Many people waste an incredible amount of time and energy feeling stressed about what they cannot control. We worry about what other people do and say, things that happened in the past, the weather and numerous other matters that cannot be controlled. Instead of wasting our energy on the uncontrollable, we would be much better off focusing on factors we can control.

Self-awareness

A first step towards knowing what skills need to be developed is self-awareness. How do we know what to correct if we do not know what we are currently doing? Although there are multiple approaches to self-awareness, two of them will be addressed here. The first is the use of self-evaluation forms by athletes, the second is their knowledge of their optimal mental state for peak performance.

In Chapter 1 a simple self-evaluation form was presented. Just as self-evaluation forms are beneficial for coaches, they are also beneficial for athletes. To help your athletes become more aware of themselves (and also to help them remember some of the information you give them), it is useful to create a self-evaluation form for your athletes to complete. Even young athletes can benefit from very simple forms, for example using drawings of faces that range from a big grin to a big frown to evaluate how they are performing. Although young athletes may not differentiate between trying hard and performing well, rating their performance helps them become aware of what they are doing.

The skills, characteristics or elements that you include on a form serve as reminders of the points on which you want your athletes to focus. The more advanced your athletes, the more detailed the form needs to be. In addition, rather than having responses to scales range from '5 = excellent' to '1 = poor', more precise information can be included. For example, if you were interested in having athletes rate their peripheral vision, you could have the rating scale range from '5 = reads play, very aware' to '1 = tunnel vision, unaware of surroundings'.

The factors to be included on a self-evaluation form are only limited by your imagination. Examples of elements that could be included are:

- aspects of fitness (speed, power or endurance)
- sport-specific technical skills (blocking, serving or kicking)
- mental skills (confidence, concentration or arousal control)
- social skills (leadership, supporting teammates or calling for the ball)
- game play (anticipation, decision-making and sticking to the game plan).

Once again, the younger or more novice the athletes, the simpler the form. Only a few minutes should be needed to complete the forms. Most of the questions should involve circling a rating. Including a couple of open-ended questions, however, can be useful. For example, a question about what they want to remember for the next training session or competition may help them recall an important teaching point. Asking them to state one thing they did really well that day can help them focus on the positive. When self-confidence is lagging, reading back over all the great things they have previously accomplished is uplifting.

ACTIVITY

What were the three things you most wanted your athletes to achieve or remember as a result of your most recent training session?

1.

2.

3.

Now for each of those factors/elements, describe good and poor execution or performance.

Factor/Element	Good	Poor
Example: Batting placement	Found space	Found fielder

Continuing this process, you can begin to create an athlete self-evaluation form for your sport. An example of a self-evaluation form for an experienced volleyball team follows:

Enhancing Performance with Mental Skills 139

Player: _____ Date: _____ Venue: _____

Skill	Elements	Key		Rating
Serving	Preparation	Rushed	Deliberate	1 2 3 4 5
	Accuracy	Frequent errors	Hit target	1 2 3 4 5
	Tactics	No plan	Selected options	1 2 3 4 5
	After serve	Too slow	Quickly in position	1 2 3 4 5
Reception	Anticipation	Not ready/late	Early position	1 2 3 4 5
	Footwork	Nil/clumsy	Smooth/balanced	1 2 3 4 5
	Arm position	Late preparation	Good platform	1 2 3 4 5
	Movement	Jerky/disjointed	Smooth/co-ordinated	1 2 3 4 5
	Touch	Tense/hard	Soft/smooth	1 2 3 4 5
	Accuracy	No control	Consistent to target	1 2 3 4 5
Setting	Footwork	Late/off balance	Under ball/balanced	1 2 3 4 5
	Body position	Back to net	Square to target	1 2 3 4 5
	Touch	Hard/tense	Soft/smooth	1 2 3 4 5
	Accuracy	Sprays sets	Consistent zone	1 2 3 4 5
	Set selection	Guess/no plan	Selected best option	1 2 3 4 5
Hitting	Contact point	Low	High	1 2 3 4 5
	Power	Weak	Strong	1 2 3 4 5
	Success rate	Lots of errors	Lots of kills	1 2 3 4 5
	Reading block	Not aware	Good vision	1 2 3 4 5
Blocking	Anticipation	No idea	Read play well	1 2 3 4 5
	Hands	Soft	Hard/thumbs up	1 2 3 4 5
	Penetration	Hands off net	Good reach	1 2 3 4 5
Defence	Attitude	Whimped out	Committed	1 2 3 4 5
	Anticipation	Guessed	Aware of positions	1 2 3 4 5
	Court position	Out of position	In position	1 2 3 4 5
	Body position	Too high/on heels	Weight forward	1 2 3 4 5
Mental	Confidence	Easily intimidated	Believed in ability	1 2 3 4 5
		Tentative	Decisive	1 2 3 4 5
	Concentration	Easily distracted	Remained focused	1 2 3 4 5
	Determination	Gave up	Hung in there	1 2 3 4 5

Two keys to remember for next time: _____

_____

Highlight: _____

Providing a few minutes at the end of training sessions for athletes to complete self-evaluation forms indicates to your athletes that you believe it is an important activity. If you just ask them to complete the forms sometime before you see them next they will perceive that you do not think the forms are important enough to use training time. In addition, the longer they wait to complete them, the less accurate their responses will be.

Another technique for increasing self-awareness is to help athletes determine how they need to be to perform their best (i.e. their optimal mental state). Do they need to be relaxed, excited, thinking about their technique, focused on the feeling of movement, or nervous? An estimate can be made by thinking back to past performances, but a more accurate understanding can be obtained by keeping diaries.

If you are just familiarising athletes with the concept, have them think about two performances they have had in the past; one where they individually performed very well and one when they did not perform as well as expected. Avoid selecting performances that were influenced by illness, injury, or major equipment failure. Then have them write down everything they can remember about what they were thinking and how they were feeling before and during each performance. Most athletes will discover that their thoughts and feelings were different for the two performances.

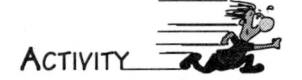

ACTIVITY

Think back over your performances as a coach. Avoiding situations when you may have been sick or injured, select a time when you think you performed very well as a coach and another when you did not perform to your expectations. Write down a few facts that will remind you of the specific situations, for example, where you were, when it was, or anything memorable that occurred. Then write down everything you can remember about what you were thinking or how you were feeling both before and during those two performances.

Positive Experience	Negative Experience
Description:	Description:
Thoughts and feelings:	Thoughts and feelings:

Are there any differences between the positive and negative performances in terms of what you were thinking and how you were feeling?

In most cases, our best performances are where we are focused on what it is we are doing and when we are feeling confident, in control and at our optimal level of arousal. Individual differences, however, do exist. Some people may perform poorly when feeling too confident as their overconfidence is really false confidence, such as the feeling that 'I'm so great I don't need to try'. As mentioned earlier in this chapter, some people need to feel relaxed and others need to feel nervous. Similarly, some individuals need to focus on specific aspects of technique or strategy, whereas others prefer focusing on the feeling of movement or looking at the big picture.

Obviously a more accurate reflection about thoughts and feelings can be obtained if they are recorded immediately after performances instead of days, weeks, or months after the fact. Whether recording the thoughts and feelings in a diary or retrospectively remembering past performances, the idea is to determine how each individual should be thinking and feeling to obtain consistently good performances. With practice, individuals can learn to control thoughts and feelings.

Setting Goals

The goal-setting process (see Chapter 5) should not be a procedure that is entirely removed from training. If you are aware of your athletes' goals, you can try to incorporate some of their strategies for achieving their goals into the design of your training sessions. In addition, athletes can improve their concentration and level of effort in drills if they set specific goals for each training session or even for specific drills. Coaches often set goals for their athletes during training by saying that a certain number of successful attempts should be made before moving onto the next drill. Getting the athletes to set these goals will make them more committed to the activity.

SELF-REFLECTION

Watch 30 minutes of a video of one of your training sessions and answer the following questions:

- Which of your athletes' goals did you have in mind when planning this section of training?
- Did you either refer to their goals during the session or question your athletes about how activities related to their goals?
- Did you incorporate goal setting into any particular activities or drills? Did you set the goals or did you allow your athletes to set the goals?
- How might you better incorporate goal setting in your future training sessions?

Controlling Arousal

Earlier in this chapter you did an activity that asked you to rate your optimal level of arousal for various activities. You used a scale of 1 to 10, with '1' being sluggish, as if you had just woken up, and '10' being the most activated you have ever been in your life (with the adrenalin really pumping). Familiarise your athletes with the scale and get them to think about where on the scale they should be for different technical skills or activities. Then, during training sessions (and competitions) you can periodically ask them where they are on the scale. If their ratings are lower or higher than they should be, they can then learn to raise or lower their arousal levels. Although the term 'arousal' is usually used in the literature, you may want to refer to 'activation levels' instead of 'arousal levels', particularly if you are working with teenagers. Adolescents have the tendency to read sex into everything and may find talking about arousal embarrassing.

There are many techniques that can be used to control arousal (activation) levels. Space limitations do not allow for an in-depth description of this area. (See the books listed at the end of this chapter for more help.) However, to give you some idea about what can be done, examples of techniques for raising and lowering arousal (activation) levels are provided.

Raising Arousal (increasing activation)

Athletes (and coaches) can use very simple techniques to raise their arousal levels. Under-arousal can be a problem at training sessions, particularly if they are early in the morning or late in the day after a full day of study or work. Often just increasing activity level helps wake people up and makes them feel more like training. This can easily be done by incorporating fun (and sometimes silly) games at the beginning of training. For example, different versions of tag are often more engaging than simply running laps to warm up (see Chapter 4). Depending on where you train and the age of your athletes, you might also consider having team screams as a way of increasing activation. Having everyone yell at the top of their lungs for 15 to 20 seconds definitely serves as a wake-up call. Another option is playing fast-paced and relatively loud music at the beginning of training. You can use the privilege of selecting the music as part of your reward system. If individual athletes seem a bit slack in their attitude towards training, reminding them of their goals can increase their intensity.

Lowering Arousal (decreasing activation)

A multitude of relaxation methods exist. Abdominal breathing is an example of a technique that can help with relaxation as well as concentration. The easiest way for you (and your athletes) to learn the technique is to lie down on your back with your legs uncrossed (if you have back trouble, put your feet and lower legs up on a chair). Place one hand on your stomach, just below your belly button and then rest the other hand gently on top.

- Inhale so that your stomach and hands rise as you breathe in.
- Exhale so that your stomach and hands fall as you breathe out.
- Try to spend the same amount of time breathing in as you do breathing out.
- Try to make the transition between the two as natural as possible as if your breathing has a mind of its own.
- If other thoughts come into your head, stop and refocus on your breathing. Some find it useful to thank the thoughts for making themselves known and then letting them float on through.
- Continue breathing in this manner, but now every time you exhale repeat the word 'relax' silently to yourself.

- If other thoughts come into your head, refocus on your breathing, saying the word 'relax'.

You may want to replace the word 'relax' with a different concentration word or cue. Trevor, a coach, uses the cue 'temper' to remind himself to keep his cool as he has the tendency to lose his patience when coaching. Yvonne, an athlete, uses the word 'rhubarb'. Rhubarb has nothing to do with her sport, but there was a joke in her family about rhubarb and thinking about it makes her relax and reminds her to have fun. Jane, a volleyball player, uses the cue 'thumbs up' when she is in front court to remind her about correct blocking technique. As you can see, the options are unlimited.

At first spend about 6–10 minutes on this exercise each day. Eventually decrease the time to 3–5 minutes. You should also change your position from lying down to sitting, to standing and then eventually to a position that is relevant to your sport. For example, Jerry, a surfer, practises abdominal breathing using his cue word as if he is straddling his board. No matter what your sport is, you have to breathe while you participate. With the possible exception of underwater hockey, using breathing with a cue word can be applied at any time during training or competition.

ACTIVITY

To help your athletes discover cue words that might be useful, give four words for each topic listed below that might be relevant for your sport.

Topic				
Speed	*fast*	*dash*	*quick*	*fly*
Strength				
Timing				
Power				
Form				
Movement				
Rhythm				
Persistence				
Quality				
Concentration				
Emotion				
Other				

Self-talk/Self-confidence

The cue words used to help control arousal (activation) levels also help to control self-talk. That little voice in our heads cannot be reminding us of our past mistakes if we are engaging that voice in repeating cue words. The easiest way to control self-talk is to have something positive or constructive to think about.

In addition to cue words, we can use positive affirmations to control our self-talk. Positive affirmations are just positive self-statements that can remind us of our strengths and abilities. Examples of positive affirmations include statements such as 'I am well-prepared for this training session'; 'I am very persistent, I always keep trying'; 'I am quick'; and 'I can adapt to changing conditions'. If we are thinking about what we are capable of doing, we cannot at the same time also be thinking about our weaknesses or concerns. Positive affirmations are only useful if we can agree, at least in part, with the statement. For this reason, it is imperative for individuals to create their own lists of positive affirmations. As you coach, you can create your own affirmations, as well as have your athletes write their own affirmations.

ACTIVITY

Write down 10 positive affirmations. If you have trouble thinking of positive statements, think back to the last time you did something that made you feel good about yourself or the times when others have complimented you. Even if you do not perform a particular behaviour 100 per cent of the time, you can still turn it into a positive affirmation because if you have done something even once, you know you have the ability to do it again. For example, if you have tended to lose your temper in the past, but are learning to control it, you could use the positive affirmation, 'I am capable of controlling my emotions'.

1.

2.

3.

4.

5.

6.

7.

8.

9.

10.

Now check back through the list you have written and ensure that all the statements are worded in the positive. For example, use 'I can control my emotions' instead of, 'I don't lose my temper'. Also, check that all of the statements are about you – your characteristics, abilities, skills or competencies. For this activity to be most effective, you should now record your statements onto an audiotape. It may take you four or five takes until your voice sounds convincing and believable. Some athletes prefer recording their statements over background music that they like to listen to before competition. The tape can then be played before competition or at times when a confidence boost is needed. Obviously, the tapes should always be the personal property of the individual for use in personal stereos rather than public address systems.

Self-confidence can also be enhanced by applying strategies that have been discussed previously. For example, setting and achieving goals, attaining an optimal level of arousal and reviewing highlights, either from videos or self-evaluation forms, can all strengthen self-confidence. Imagery can also help develop self-confidence.

Using Imagery

Athletes can use imagery to see and feel themselves performing the way they want. Using imagery to remind themselves of previous good performances can enhance their confidence. As mentioned earlier in this chapter, imagery can also increase how quickly athletes learn new skills. However, for imagery to be effective, it needs to be controlled.

You can help athletes control their imagery by developing imagery scripts. Writing (and then recording) scripts that indicate what a skill should feel like when being performed correctly allows athletes to follow your suggestions. Until athletes develop control of imagery, it is difficult for them to just close their eyes and instantly create an appropriate image of a skill or situation. When creating an imagery script, include as many of the senses as you can, be sure you word everything in the positive and finish the script with a statement similar to, 'and now repeat the image in normal time'. Images need to be repeated in normal time because it takes longer to describe the performance of a skill than it does to actually do it. If athletes only create images in slow motion as when following a script, they may end up performing that skill in slow motion as well.

ACTIVITY

Choose a physical skill or strategy from your sport that athletes sometimes have difficulty performing correctly. Write an imagery script for that skill. It is useful to get feedback about your script from others who are familiar with your sport. Refining and revising scripts as well as adding to your repertoire can be an ongoing process.

In addition to providing imagery scripts, you can also incorporate imagery into your training sessions by having your athletes create 'instant replays'. When athletes perform a skill correctly, have them stop and recreate, in their minds, exactly what they just did, by focusing on the feel of the correct performance and instantly replaying it in their minds. It is as if they are making a video of that performance that they can then take out and play whenever they want. Without instant replays, asking athletes to remember how they performed a skill the previous week is usually ineffective. Athletes often forget what they did differently to improve their technique. By using instant replay, even if they do not understand exactly what it is they changed, they can remind themselves of the feeling of correct performance and thereby increase the chances of repeating that correct performance.

Concentration/Attention

Some ideas for improving attention were presented in Chapter 3. The cue words discussed in this chapter, in addition to helping with optimal arousal and self-talk, also help individuals focus on relevant aspects of performance. Cues relating to technique, form, timing or concentration help athletes focus on what it is they need to do to perform effectively.

DEVELOPING CONCENTRATION.

Another very simple exercise that can easily be incorporated into training is 'Past, Present, Future'. All it involves is calling out once or twice a session, 'Past, present or future'. The idea is for athletes to stop right then and determine whether they were thinking about the past, the present or the future. Ideally, athletes would spend the majority of training (and competition) thinking about the present, what they are actually doing at that point in time. Unfortunately, some athletes get less out of training because they are thinking about the past (the mistake they made 10 minutes ago, or the argument they had with a friend before training) or the future (what they are going to have to eat when they get home or an assignment they need to complete).

Simulations

Simulating competition conditions during training is an excellent method of preparing athletes mentally as well as physically. It is a great way of integrating mental and physical skills. Simulations can also be used to familiarise athletes with the use of each skill in different situations. Examples of simulation follow:

- Simulating a noisy crowd by playing a tape of crowd noise at training.
- Simulating rainy conditions by training with the hose on or the sprinklers and/or using balls from a bucket of water.
- Simulating competition times by training at the same time the athletes will be competing (for example, late at night or early in the morning).
- Simulating competition surfaces by training on a variety of surfaces.
- Simulating competitive situations by practising coming from behind. Similarly, it can be useful to practise situations where the athletes are well in front, or where competition is very even.
- Simulating specific offensive or defensive situations.

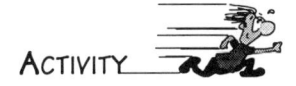

ACTIVITY

Plan how you could introduce three different types of simulations in training:

1.

2.

3.

Summary

1. Mental skills can help athletes and coaches achieve better and more consistent performances.
2. Mental skills not only aid performance enhancement, they also help people enjoy their participation in sport and can be useful in many situations outside of sport.

3. Mental skills require practice.
4. Athletes need to learn how to focus on important cues and ignore irrelevant information or distractions.
5. Performance can be less than optimal if arousal levels are too high or too low.
6. Imagery needs to be vivid and controlled to be effective.
7. Realistic and constructive positive self-talk can help focus attention and increase confidence.
8. The main point of mental skills it to help individuals control the controllable.
9. Self-evaluation forms help athletes become more aware of themselves and can serve as reminders of the points on which you want the athletes to focus.
10. Determining how to 'be' to perform one's best can be achieved by reflecting on past performances – both good and bad.
11. The first step of arousal control is for each individual to determine his or her optimal level of arousal for different skills and activities.
12. Music, yelling and active games can help athletes raise their arousal levels. Abdominal breathing can be used to lower arousal levels.
13. Cue words can help control arousal levels and self-talk as well as help individuals focus on relevant aspects of performance.
14. Using imagery as a reminder of previous good performances can enhance confidence. You can help athletes control their imagery by developing imagery scripts.
15. Simulating competition conditions during training is an excellent method of preparing athletes mentally as well as physically.

Further Reading

Orlick, T. (1986), *Psyching for Sport: Mental Training for Athletes*, Champaign, IL: Leisure.
Orlick, T. (1986), *Coaches' Training Manual to Psyching for Sport*, Champaign, IL: Leisure.
Syer, J. and Connolly, C. (1984), *Sporting Body Sporting Mind*, Cambridge: Cambridge University.
Williams, J.M. (ed.) (1993), *Applied Sport Psychology: Personal Growth to Peak Performance* (2nd ed.), Mountain View, CA: Mayfield.

Chapter 9

Coaching During Competitions

- Developing a Pre-competition Routine
- Developing a Competition Plan
- Self-control
- Extra Jobs when Travelling with a Team

Chapter 8 finished with the suggestion that coaches should simulate competition conditions during training. In some respects, the opposite should happen during competitions. Athletes usually feel confident and comfortable during training sessions. Therefore, when athletes can feel that the skills and circumstances of competition are similar to those of training, they tend to be more relaxed and perform better. For example, when shooting a free throw in basketball in the final moments of a close game, athletes will usually benefit from reminding themselves that it is the exact same action as that done in training thousands of times before.

The simplest method to ensure that athletes approach performance in competition the same way as they do in training is to help them develop mental plans. Experienced, élite athletes have a consistent base to their performances and behaviours. They use well-learned and consistent routines that they execute each and every time they train and compete. If athletes want to produce a consistent, high-quality performance every time they compete, then they need to have a consistent base from which to perform. This base includes consistency in technique, fitness and psychological or behavioural routines.

If athletes have a consistent base from which to perform, they feel more confident and maintain better control of timing, concentration, thought processes, mental rehearsal, reactions to pressure and emotional states. If something happens that has the potential to distract their preparation or concentration during performance, they will be more likely to recover quickly and refocus if they have good mental plans. Well-prepared athletes recover quickly from distraction and find it easy to maintain focus on task-relevant, positive aspects of performance because they have a plan to stick to. Mental plans include both a pre-competition routine as well as a competition plan.

Developing a Pre-competition Routine

A pre-competition routine should strengthen the feeling of being prepared and therefore increase athletes' confidence. Prior to competition athletes and coaches should avoid self-defeating thoughts that tend to lead to worry, poor confidence, interference with concentration and less enjoyment. Pre-competition routines should help athletes and coaches enter into a desirable pre-event feeling, activation level and focus of attention.

As the coach, you can help athletes to create their own pre-competition routines. You may provide a basic structure that they then fill in to best suit their individual requirements. A pre-competition routine will include elements of both physical warm-up and psychological warm-up. Most people are familiar with aspects of physical warm-up, but are unaware of what a psychological warm-up might entail.

A psychological-warm-up usually includes a combination of structured self-talk, imagery and sometimes music. Self-talk should take the form of realistic positive self-suggestions such as reminders of preparation, readiness, ability, adaptability, commitment, intensity and positiveness. Imagery can be calming or activating (depending on the required level of arousal) and typically includes reminders of the competition plan, past personal bests or good training sessions and the feeling of executing the first few moves perfectly. Music is sometimes included as part of a psychological warm-up as certain songs may help create the preferred pre-competition state of mind.

The final element of a pre-competition routine is a pre-start focus (the focus of attention just before the start of competition). The pre-start focus can include a brief reminder of the competition plan, final adjustment of arousal level and the focus on the first few movements.

When athletes create a pre-competition routine they can draw upon the feelings and thoughts that served them best in the past. An example of a generic pre-competition routine follows:

- Arrive at venue XX minutes before the start
- Check equipment
- Begin stretching and warm-up
- Think happy, relaxed thoughts
- Positively image up-coming performance
- Listen to coach's comments
- Apply these comments to imagery
- Engage in heavier physical preparation
- Use more imagery if needed
- Engage in quicker physical activity
- Ready self for the start – think of opening skills
- Cue word for the first skill.

ACTIVITY

Create a blueprint that your athletes could use to develop a pre-competition routine. If you coach young children or novices, the routine should be fairly simple. If you coach older or more experienced athletes you can make the routine more complex.

Having a structured pre-competition routine is only part of the mental planning required to produce consistent performances. Being properly prepared for competition just gets athletes started. They also need to be able to maintain their focus during competition. A competition plan is the second facet of mental plans.

Developing a Competition Plan

A competition plan should help athletes focus on the most appropriate cues during the competition. The plan should also help athletes get back on track if they are distracted, make an error, or just have their attention drift. Basically, competition plans are a compilation of cue words (as mentioned in Chapter 8). The make-up of the plan will, in part, be determined by the type of sport.

For team sports such as rugby, soccer or hockey, the competition focus plan should break down the sport into specific skills or critical situations. For example there can be a team strategy about what to focus on just after the opposition has scored. Short races or routines such as those involved in sprinting, throwing, diving or gymnastics can involve sequential checkpoints that remind the athletes of specific technical cues. Long events such as marathons can have general cues or reminders that can be used throughout the event whenever the athletes need to maintain focus. For example, cues relating to technique, arousal, or self-encouragement could be used when experiencing signs of fatigue, when approaching a big hill, or after being passed.

The specific cues used in a competition focus plan will depend on the athletes' personalities, their level of performance, their past experience and the sport itself. When creating a plan, athletes will have to decide how they want to feel, focus and function during the phases of competition. Words and phrases that appear in the self-evaluation forms you created for your athletes as well as the activities in Chapter 8 regarding cue words and positive affirmations can all be sources of cues for competition plans.

Two examples of competition plans follow. Note how they can be sequential or situational. In addition, cue phrases that initially are lengthy can be shortened over time and retain their full meaning.

100m sprint (track)		
Segment	**Cue**	**Purpose**
0-30 m	'push'	acceleration phase
30-60 m	'heel'	maximum velocity stage
60-100 m	'claw'	speed endurance phase

Volleyball		
Situation or Skill	**Cue**	**Shortened Cue**
Serving	'take your time'	'time'
Receiving serve	'want to be served to'	'want it'
Setting	'make position'	'position'
Hitting	'high elbow'	'elbow'
Blocking	'thumbs up'	'thumbs'
Back court	'on toes, weight forward'	'toes'
Other team scored	'ready for next serve'	'ready'

ACTIVITY

Create a draft competition plan that could be used as an example for your athletes. Although individual athletes may find certain cues to be more beneficial than others, a draft plan can provide them with a starting point.

Situation or Skill	Cue	Shortened Cue

Once competition plans are developed, verbally reminding athletes of cues during competition is usually much more useful than providing a long-winded explanation of what the athletes should be doing. Coaches can also benefit from having pre-competition routines and competition plans. For example, a tennis coach might have as his or her pre-competition routine the following:

- Choose a team space (claim an area for a team base)
- Verify opponents, courts and times
- Check on practice courts (if available) and organise times
- Check that the players are happy and starting their own pre-competition routines
- Timetable pre-match talks at times that suit the players
- Hold pre-match talks and/or warm-ups.

Self-control

Competition is not the time to overload athletes with information or the place to introduce new strategies or techniques. Although opportunities for coaching input vary by sport, the coaching that can actually be done during competitions is minimal. Even though athletes can learn from competition, the competitive situation is not the appropriate place for vast amounts of instruction.

As mentioned in Chapter 3, the anxiety of athletes increases when importance is placed on the outcome and/or when they feel uncertain about their ability, training, place on the team, or any other aspect of performance. One of the most common competitive coaching errors is to place great importance on the outcome of specific competitions. It is not unusual to hear comments such as, 'this event is what you have been training all year for', 'the upcoming game is the most important game of your life', or 'remember, the selectors will be watching this weekend, be sure to perform your absolute best'. Even young children recognise the importance of elimination matches, grand finals and selection trials. Reminding them of this importance only serves to place greater pressure on them, usually resulting in increased anxiety and self-doubt and poorer performance.

Some coaches feel compelled to pull out all the stops when it comes to a grand final or an unusually important competition. Instead of sticking with routines and behaviours that worked to get the players or competitors to where they are, they decide that fancier methods are required. No major changes should be made before or during major competitions. Things should remain as familiar as possible. Even if a particular behaviour is less than optimal, suddenly changing that behaviour before a competition usually has worse consequences than persisting with the original course of action. For example, if athletes are junk food junkies, changing their diet to healthy meals and snacks would be a beneficial change in the long run. However, if the change was made immediately prior to a major competition, those concerned not only may have physiological reactions to the change in diet, they may also feel out of sorts because things are different. They are no longer in their comfort zone and feel that things are not quite right.

Coaching during competitions can be frustrating as coaches have limited control at this stage in terms of how their athletes perform. In reality, coaches can often do more harm than good during competition. The previous paragraphs mentioned the anxiety of athletes, but it needs to be noted that coaches get anxious as well. The main difference is that coaches' anxiety can be compounded by their sense of having little or no control. Studies have shown that the heart rate and blood pressure of coaches on the sidelines can exceed that of the athletes out running around.

Just as athletes should focus on controlling the controllable, coaches should do the same. Techniques for arousal control were introduced in Chapter 8. Although when coaching you may get frustrated and be tempted to lose your temper, maintaining self-control and remembering to implement the positive coaching behaviours mentioned earlier in this book will be beneficial for your athletes. If you are nervous or anxious, your athletes will pick up on that nervousness and anxiety and become more like you. On the other hand, if you are calm, focused and positive, your athletes will tend to be the same.

THE POSITIVE APPROACH IS FOR COMPETITION AS WELL AS TRAINING.

Point to Remember

You have done all you can do to prepare your athletes for competitions. If you have not, then it is too late to prepare them during competitions. Enjoy the competitions and learn from what occurs. The positive approach is for competition as well as training.

SELF-REFLECTION

For this practice you will need to have videotapes of yourself coaching during competitions. Observe yourself coaching during competitions. The following reflective questions are designed to help you determine how your behaviour and attitude affect your athletes.

- How confident do you appear to be of your athletes?
- Do you demonstrate any signs of anxiety?
- Do you remain positive even when your athletes are not performing as well as you may have expected or hoped?
- Does it look like you are enjoying yourself and that you really want to be there?
- Do you provide your athletes with cue words or phrases?
- Have you avoided the pitfall of information overload?
- How enthusiastic do you seem to be?
- Does your frustration show, or were you able to control it?
- Are you smiling?

Now select two behaviours that you could improve during competitions. State specifically what you are going to try to do that is different from what you are currently doing.

Behaviour	Specific Improvements

Extra Jobs when Travelling with a Team

Coaches are often required to perform administrative or managerial functions when travelling with a team or being involved with a team during a weekend-long competition. Those duties may include looking after travel, equipment, alternative activities, food and assorted other requirements.

Travel Arrangements

Making individual athletes responsible for travel arrangements not only decreases opportunities for developing team cohesion that can be achieved when travelling or staying together as a unit, it can also result in athletes arriving at the wrong place at the wrong time. Coaches may want to be involved in activities such as determining the condition of the vehicle used for travel (petrol, spare tyre, oil); knowing exactly where the competition venue is; verifying reservations for accommodation, cars, shuttles, or planes; confirming departure and arrival times; and checking any required documentation such as registration forms, passports or visas.

Equipment

It is important to check all equipment early enough to fix anything that might not be right. Assigning specific individuals to be responsible for different items such as drink bottles, uniforms, balls, first aid supplies or sunscreen can give athletes a greater sense of responsibility as well as help share the workload. Providing athletes with a checklist of equipment and personal gear they should bring can aid in ensuring the necessary gear is brought with the athletes.

COACHES OFTEN NEED TO PLAY MANY ROLES WHEN TRAVELLING WITH A TEAM.

Filling Time

Groups of excited young athletes can result in major headaches for the coach if careful consideration has not been given to what the athletes will do when they are not actually competing. Requiring participants to bring books, cards or computer games is a useful first step. If large blocks of time need to be filled, it can be beneficial to establish in advance team activities that are fun but do not sap all the energy from the athletes. Check the venue and ask organisers to provide information about local attractions.

Food

Prior to departing for longer-term competitions, the coach needs to establish what the meal arrangements will be. Age, experience, cooking facilities and financial considerations will determine whether individual athletes will be responsible for supplying their own food, everyone will chip in to buy food and then take turns cooking, the team will eat out, a parent or manager will serve the role of full-time cook, or a combination of these methods will be used. When planning food, remember to include water and other liquids as a form of rehydration. If you are planning to shop for food, it is useful to plan menus, so that shopping can be made easier on the pocket as well as the shopper.

Being Ten People at Once

Travelling with teams often requires coaches to fill a variety of roles at the same time. Only experience and practice can tell you which hat(s) to wear when, but you can be sure that multiple credentials will be required. These roles include (but are not limited to): mother, physiologist, nurse, doctor, chauffeur, physiotherapist, psychologist, father and friend. Be prepared for minimal sleep.

Summary

1. When athletes can feel that the skills and circumstances of competition are similar to those of training, they tend to be more relaxed and perform better.
2. Mental plans, including pre-competition routines and competition plans give athletes a consistent base from which to perform.
3. Pre-competition routines should help athletes enter into a desirable pre-event feeling, activation level and focus of attention.
4. Competition plans should help athletes focus on the most appropriate cues during the competition and help them get back on track if they are distracted.
5. Verbally reminding athletes of cues from their competition plans is an effective coaching behaviour.
6. During competitions, coaches need to maintain self-control and remember to implement positive coaching behaviours.
7. Coaches are often required to perform administrative or managerial functions when travelling with a team.

Further Reading

Mallett, C. and Hanrahan, S.J. (in press), 'Race Modelling: An Effective Cognitive Strategy for the 100m Sprinter?', *The Sport Psychologist*.

Orlick, T. (1986), *Psyching for Sport: Mental Training for Athletes*, Champaign, IL: Leisure Press.

Section IV

Factors Influencing Coaching

Chapter 10

Parents

- A Coach–Parents Meeting
- Communication During the Season
- Expectations of Parents

We include a chapter on parents here because parents are often very influential and provide a source of support and/or stress for junior athletes. We often hear negative stories about what parents have and have not done on the sidelines during competitions and even during training, but there are also lots of positive behaviours that provide the support necessary for children to participate.

Children begin participating in organised sport as young as five years of age. At this young age, parents play a major role in the decisions about their children's participation. Not many five-year-olds ask their parents if they can play sport. So, parents play a major role in encouraging children to play sport.

> **POINT TO PONDER**
> Recent parental influences on children's sport have been made evident in the media. In Dunedin, an incident occurred where a parent tripped an opposition player in rugby because the player was about to tackle his son who was on his way to score a try (*Otago Daily Times*, 16 July 1994). The parent was charged and required to complete 200 hours of community service. This extreme behaviour is rare in children's sport, however, every coach, athlete, referee and parent has a story about parents' behaviours at sporting events. With such behaviour, there is a concern for the type of competitive experiences young children have.

Incidents, like the one described in 'Point to Ponder' above, have emerged as controversial in defining parental roles and expectations for youth sports. Such behaviour can have a negative impact on children's participation in sport. Negative behaviours and comments on the sidelines can cause competitive stress, inhibit sport performance and cause children to drop out of sport. There have been several instances of negative influence by parents and in some leagues, parents have been banned from spectating. This is an unfortunate circumstance because parental support can have a positive influence on children participating in sport. Parental support seems to be strong when the child does well, but parents are humans and they tend to be critical. Parents often discuss athletes' mistakes in a critical, often demeaning, rather than a positive manner. Parents naturally want their children to succeed, and may become emotional in a harmful way. There is a problem when the actions of the parents begin to be accepted by the children and both children and parents live through a world of 'distorted perceptions'. There is evidence that parental encouragement and support significantly enhance children's experience in competitive sport. Parents have a very important role in the success of children's participation in sport.

CRITICAL PARENT – TOUGH ON THE CHILD AS WELL AS THE COACH.

One way to help parents enhance the environment and decrease competitive stress is for coaches to take responsibility for educating athletes' parents. Some textbooks advocate that the people who can best deal with the parents and the different situations in sport are the coaches. This chapter provides some insight as to how coaches can influence parental behaviour. The issue of parental behaviours and their influence on children will be discussed. Guidelines on educating parents to be supportive and encouraging will be highlighted. One of the essential principles is to communicate effectively, and what better way than to hold a coach–parents meeting to discuss your philosophy and expectations for the season. Such a meeting is a great way to demonstrate and explain anecdotes about situations you have observed, so that parents may see and understand the effects of negative behaviours. Coaches can then ensure clear, consistent lines of communication throughout the season.

A Coach–Parents Meeting

A coach–parents meeting should be held at the beginning of the season and all parents should be encouraged to be present. One of the first questions coaches may ask is 'how do we get the parents of our team to this meeting'. One answer is to ensure the meeting is fun or exciting for them by making the meeting attractive. Imagine a parent saying no to this: 'Mummy, we are having a parents' meeting for our t-ball team next Monday night. It is going to be a sausage sizzle and the coach is going to provide games for us to play. She said I can't go unless I bring you, so please, please, can we go? I promised Joseph that I would come and he is bringing his Game Boy'.

Some parents will say no, but not all is lost. Coaches should contact those parents by phone to discuss the importance of the meeting or send home a special note. We all like to hear positive statements, so the coach can phone the parent and tell them how well Sarah is doing on the water polo team, for example, that she is a joy to coach and that the team needs more people like her. The objective here is to support the parents so they can support the coach.

Advantages of a Coach–Parents Meeting

There are many advantages to having such a meeting. Even if you have met these parents before on other teams or during previous seasons, a meeting to reinforce your philosophies and objectives is extremely important. The biggest advantage is the establishment of clear lines of communication. By holding this meeting the parents will be provided with an avenue to speak with the coach. One of the major concerns of parents is that they are not informed. They are generally quite keen to hear information about programmes in which their children are involved. At the meeting, coaches should help parents to understand the team rules and procedures. The coach's expectations for training should be outlined in the meeting, so it is clear to the parents the commitment that is required of each athlete. The understanding of team rules should reduce potential conflicts. If you establish rules and boundaries, the parents will be clear about your expectations. The meeting will also provide an avenue for coaches to understand parents' concerns.

The meeting will allow coaches to present their objectives of the training season. The parents will get to know you better. This is a time to inform parents of your philosophy and determine any differing views amongst the parents. If the parents are not happy with how you will approach the team, then they can look for other teams. For example, if a coach decides that the purpose of her or his team is to develop skills and there is a parent who is more concerned with winning, the coach can communicate the rationale for her or his philosophy and a method for adhering to this philosophy. The meeting provides an opportunity to discuss the differing views so that parents can make informed decisions.

The parents should be informed about the sport and its potential risks. A coach–parents meeting is a golden opportunity for coaches to discuss safety and implications of wearing protective gear. This is a major issue as coaches are responsible for athletes' safety. Parents should be informed of the sort of protective gear required and the consequences of athletes not having the gear. If the lack of protective gear can cause serious injury, the parents should be informed that their child will not participate if not supplied appropriately. A coach's first concern should be the athletes' welfare.

The meeting is a great opportunity to inform parents about the sport and its process. It is an occasion for coaches to explain or demonstrate the sport itself, so that parents have an understanding of the competition while watching. Coaches can find out which parents will be able to help conduct the season's activities, fund-raise or provide other forms of support. Many of the parents will have special talents and skills to offer the team. The meeting is a good opportunity to encourage the use of these skills to support the athletes.

It is also essential that coaches discuss their expectations of parents on the sidelines – what is acceptable behaviour and what is not. Often just holding a meeting shows how much you care about the children, but a little bit of emphasis on fair play and positive expectations helps to create a successful season on the sideline.

Conducting a Coach–Parents Meeting

One of the first considerations is when and where the meeting should be held. Ideally, choose a time when most of the parents can attend. Ensure it is as close to the start of the season as possible because the sooner you communicate with parents, the sooner a positive, supportive environment can be created. Encourage all parents to attend. If you personally invite them, they are more likely to come.

Now, that the meeting is scheduled, plan the meeting. Try not to make the meeting more than an hour long because parents and coaches are extremely busy people. The location of the meeting should be somewhere accessible, well-lit, warm and with enough space for the whole team to fit. Ensure there is a video recorder. A videotape of parents' behaviours, athletes' behaviours or even the sport is quite useful when making a personal statement. It would be appropriate to prepare name tags or have icebreaker games so the parents can get to know each other.

The athletes should attend the meeting if you are comfortable for them to do so. Sometimes having the athletes there can help remind parents of your expectations. Some coaches may feel that having their athletes there may inhibit the communication with the parents. If you coach young athletes, it may be appropriate to organise a game or activity they can do while you are meeting with the parents. If the athletes are older, they should be included in the process. It is entirely up to each coach whether or not to include the athletes.

Agenda

These are only suggestions based on some experiences that have worked, but the crucial point is to actually conduct such a meeting. One of the first items for the meeting should be an introduction. Welcome the parents to the meeting and introduce yourself. The introduction should include a bit of background about your job and then a bit about your previous coaching and sporting experience. Next, briefly describe your coaching philosophy (see Chapter 2). To help prepare for this, use your reflective techniques and consider the following questions:

- Why do athletes play your sport?
- How will athletes benefit from participating?
- What emphasis will you place on winning, on having fun and on helping the athletes to develop physically, psychologically and socially (see Chapter 4 for objectives).
- What do you expect from your players? (such as commitment, effort)
- What do you expect from the parents? (such as kind of support, encouragement)

This session should last for about 10–15 minutes (just a guideline).

For the next item on the agenda, provide a demonstration of some sort. Providing a videotape of the children practising is very valuable. It allows parents to see how their children are behaving and performing and what sorts of skills they are learning. Also, you would be surprised how many parents do not know about the sport their child is playing. Another useful video is one that shows parental behaviours on the sidelines. This video provides a background for discussion about coaches' expectations of parents. There are several commercially made videos that may be available. Contact your regional sporting organisation. Another possibility is to get the athletes to provide a live demonstration about some aspect of a skill or strategic move that they have been working on at training. This section should last for 15–20 minutes.

A useful item for the next section would be a discussion about the demonstration. If you do not provide a demonstration, then perhaps going straight into a discussion about aspects of parental behaviours and why children play sport would be useful. Remember that the main reasons that children play sport are to have fun, to be with friends, to learn and develop new skills and to experience the thrills that sport offers. Also, remember that some of the reasons children drop out are lack of fun, lack of playing time, too many criticisms, mismatched competitions and excessive anxiety (usually caused by adults who overemphasise winning). Questions to use for discussion include:

- Why do you think your child is playing sport? Have they ever dropped out of a sport? If so, why?

- How important is winning in children's sport?
- How important is having fun?
- How important is developing skills?
- What is the most important thing in youth sport?

The next item for this section may be to discuss what the role of a sport parent is. This will not be clearly defined, but you could spark some ideas by mentioning some of the good qualities of sport parents, such as keeping winning in perspective, having a healthy attitude towards sport, being a good role model, encouraging but not pressuring their child, knowing their child's goals and providing support to achieve those goals, helping their child to set realistic performance goals (see Chapter 5) and putting their child's development ahead of winning. Some questions for discussion are:

- What do you think are the most important aspects of being a supporting parent?
- Do you think there are ways that parents put pressure on children without realising it?
- How do you think parents could provide a more supportive environment for their child to achieve goals and have fun?

Another important issue to discuss is the coach's relationship with the parents. Stress open, honest communication, with parents supporting the coach when appropriate and talking to you about problems when necessary. Some questions for discussion are:

- What should coaches communicate to you – and what should you be communicating to coaches?
- What do you think a model coach–parent relationship should be like?
- What do you expect of your child's coach – and what do you think the coach should expect from you?

One of the major goals of this meeting should be to help parents do what they can to make sport fun, safe and a valuable experience for their children. Your goal as a coach is to point the parents in the right direction – by encouraging but not pushing their children, keeping winning in perspective, keeping the fun in sports, building the child's self-esteem and providing emotional as well as routine support. What makes sport a valuable experience for children is closely connected to parents' understanding of why their children like to play sport and what the role of a supporting parent should be. Be the initiator of maintaining a healthy relationship with the parents, but parents should also be encouraged to maintain a healthy relationship with the coach. Some questions to discuss are:

- Do you think that your child values sport differently than you do?
- What are the ways parents could make sport more fun for children?

This discussion section should last about 15–20 minutes.

Before opening the floor for questions and answers, inform the parents about the logistics of the sport and the expectations of the athletes. Some topics to consider include: training times, length of a season, competition details, how you will decide who plays and who does not, how frequently the team will travel, expenses for the season, fundraising, equipment needed, safety implications, rules of the team, how you will discipline the athletes, and other specific details you need to discuss.

Now that you have organised and facilitated this important meeting, allow the parents to ask further questions. Be prepared for anything here, and encourage the communication. If you cannot solve an issue that is raised, open it up for discussion to reiterate a willingness to communicate. Be sure to mention how the parents can contact you if they need to speak with you. Once questions have been answered, close the meeting. Re-emphasise some major points that have been made, such as maintaining a healthy sport perspective, encouraging but not pressuring the child and communicating effectively with the coach.

Communicating During the Season

Communication throughout the season is obviously essential to maintain or develop a good working rapport with the parents. Regular newsletters or telephone calls to inform parents of current events are essential. There will be issues that arise throughout the season – some that are expected, some that are unexpected – but coaches should be prepared to deal with them. Parents have a right to know how their son or daughter is performing or behaving. They have a right to know when the competitions are, what time training is, if there are any last-minute changes, if training or competitions have been cancelled, if their son/daughter is doing well, if their son/daughter is not doing so well, if there are injury concerns, or if the coach sees any changes that may be detrimental, such as signs of competitive stress. Parents and coaches should communicate for the betterment of the child throughout the season.

Parents want to know that their children are achieving something. They want to be reassured that their children are on track and going down the right path. Some parents want to be a part of the team more than others. By keeping the lines of communication open, coaches help to create positive, supportive parents. If they know that you care about their children, they will be happy and more co-operative. An important communication process here is letting them know good things about their children. Be honest, but give them information about their child's improvement and effort. Let them know that their child is a valued member of the team or squad.

Parents want to see how their children perform. Many parents come along to the competitions to watch their child in action. When their child does not participate, they begin to wonder and question the reasons their child is involved in the sport. Many modified sports have rules about the amount of time that athletes compete, but some coaches cut this time to the bare minimum. It is very disappointing to a parent as well as the child to participate as little as possible. Fun is participating and children participate for fun. So, if coaches have chosen not to include certain children, they must be honest and let the parents know why. If the parents know why and are still disappointed, sort out the confusion. If parents are still unhappy, do something about it, but try not to let the problem brew.

Parents also come along to competitions for social reasons. They enjoy meeting and socialising with their friends in the community. Part of the socialisation process is being able to speak with the coach, so make an extra attempt to get to know the parents' names. By showing your empathy and caring, parents will be more willing to help and provide the much-needed support.

Coaches should hold a coach–parents meeting at the start of the season. In the meeting, as described above, coaches are encouraged to communicate their expectations of parents. Once parents understand the expectations, it is the coach's responsibility to be consistent and follow through with administering the expectations. There was a rugby team in Auckland whose coach administered the rule for parents to be supportive and encouraging on the sideline. He did this by bringing out a poster that had parents' rules listed. When a parent steered away from the rule by saying negative things, the coach was there pointing to the rules and saying, 'remember our policy'. It worked well. There is also the story that was received via the Internet about a little league baseball coach who advocated the three strike rule for the season. He said that if parents were abusive or negative on the sideline, he would give them a warning (one strike), if the negative behaviour occurred a second time, the parent was asked to leave the game (two strikes). If a third negative behaviour was exhibited during the season, the coach banned the parent from coming back (third strike, you're out). Although this sounds extreme, the coach communicated his expectations to his parents and was consistent in adhering to the expectations. Consistency is the key to successful communication.

Guidelines for Successful Coach–Parent Relationships

- Ensure clear communication of your expectations to the parents.
- Be sure to be supportive and encouraging, yet firm with parents.
- Be clear on the parents' roles for the team or squad.
- Be firm and tough if parents get out of line. (Remember sport is for the benefit of the athletes.)
- Set performance guidelines for parents.
- Coach the parents.
- Keep self-control by keeping your emotions in balance. When the coach is out of control, the goals and objectives that have been set become impossible to achieve
- Include parents in supportive roles.
- Avoid conflict with parents as it is detrimental to the children.
- Remember that parental behaviour will not change quickly. Be patient, consistent, persistent and firm.

Expectations of Parents

One of the biggest reasons parents have a negative impact in sport is the pressure that they place on their children. Parents have different ideas and expectations of their children in sports. Some may motivate their children to do well because they may feel that they missed out when they were young. Others gain glory from their children's success. Most parents do not understand their own motivations for encouraging their children to participate. They may seem selfish, but this selfishness is unconscious. Parental ambition sometimes exceeds that of the child, to a point where children participate in a particular sport as a duty rather than a pleasure. These are the children who may drop out of sports.

PARENT EXPECTATIONS.

Negative parental behaviours can cause competitive stress, inhibit sport performance and cause children to drop out of sport. Competitive stress is evident by an athlete's negative reaction to a situation. There has been some evidence that parental encouragement and support significantly enhances children's experience in competitive sport. Parents have exceptionally important roles in the success of children's participation in sport. In a study that examined competitive stress, it was indicated that wrestling competitors (boys aged 9–14) who experienced greater parental pressure to participate were more likely to have pre-match stress. Boys who felt their parents and coaches were more satisfied with their wrestling performance and who perceived more positive adult involvement and interactions in the sport context experienced greater enjoyment than their counterparts with fewer positive perceptions. Coaches should be aware of these pressures and look for warning signs. The following is a list of pressures that parents sometimes place on their children:

- Guilt pressure – Sometimes parents motivate their child to participate through guilt, which increases pressure on children. An example of this is when the athlete is made to feel guilty when they are not doing well or do not achieve the goals of the parents. In this example, parents tend to provide pressure by saying 'that is not good enough, you need to work harder'.
- Financial or investment pressure – This pressure comes from parents who declare to the child consistently that they have sacrificed much to provide the financial support for the child. The child is made to feel guilty for the amount of time, money and energy parents have supposedly sacrificed so that their child can succeed.
- Sacrifice pressure – Parents claim that they have given up their happiness and life to help the child become the best athlete.
- Tension pressure – Some parents assume that pressure is good for their child, so they purposely pressure the child to force them to work harder. This form of pressure can be unrealistic as the child may not achieve certain goals.
- Living through their child pressure – This pressure is placed on the child by the parent who would like to have their child succeed in sports or skills in which the parent did not. These sorts of parents are ones that may not have been good, or not achieved a sporting goal and want their child to do it for them.
- Family identity pressure – This pressure comes from having a family of great athletes. There is pressure to be as good as or better than the family member who has achieved in the past, or there is pressure to be as good as or better than siblings.
- Self-worth pressure – This pressure comes from parents who take away love and affection when certain goals are not achieved. An example is a mother saying to her child 'I won't love you if you don't get a home run'. Self-esteem is a quality essential to all human beings, so a parent who puts on such pressure can take away self-esteem very easily.

This list of pressuring behaviours is provided so that you, as coaches, can look for signs from parents who are placing such undue pressure on their children. To enhance the safety and positive sporting environment, it is essential to continue to monitor the athletes and determine if there are excessive pressures being placed upon them. Some signs of competitive stress are irritability, tiredness, lethargy and constant injury. If an athlete has changed, look into the sorts of competitive stress that may be placed on him or her.

Points to Ponder
I've seen pushy parents in every sport and the results are generally bad. The kids that are pressured to play sport usually get sick of it and are disgusted with it for that reason. They decide to do something else.

(Arnold Palmer)

> Part of the problem with sport today is that the parents want the kids to be what they weren't and are trying to live through them. There's a difference between encouraging and standing behind versus pushing, and when the kids get old enough to make a choice, they give it away because they've been pushed so hard.
>
> (Heather McKay)

Should Parents Coach their Own Children?

The answer to this is unequivically no. There are several reasons why parents should not coach their own children. The two most important are 1) coaches could be seen to favour their own children in managing behaviours, picking teams, and other important factors in sport, and 2) coaches think that other people feel that they are favouring their child and therefore compensate for this (to the detriment of their child) providing less support for their child than for others.

Coaching your own child is a 'no-win' situation. Communication has been sighted as the major downfall when coaching your own child. As we have mentioned throughout this book, it is important for coaches to communicate equitably with all athletes and also communicate at the athletes' level. If this communication is unsuccessful, you will fail in coaching and will probably disrupt your family life as well. Even if you do manage to be fair and equitable, you will probably be perceived as either biased towards your child or unfairly harsh with your child. There are more negative than positive experiences in stories we hear about parents coaching their own children. This book advocates that parents should not coach their own children for the sake of the children on the team or squad, as well as for their own son/daughter, their family life and their own peace of mind.

POINT TO PONDER
Remember the coach who would only let his or her child play, even though others were much better or offered more team support? What about the child who always got to be in his or her favourite position because his mother was coaching?

SELF-REFLECTION

If you are considering coaching your own child or children, reflect on the following questions to help you make a more informed decision:

- What are the most significant problems you can foresee in coaching your own child?
- What are the most likely conflicts?

- What can you do to avoid or solve these potential conflicts?
- Can you communicate with your child honestly? Sport may improve the quality of your relationship with your child, or it may destroy it.
- Does your child really want to play sports? If so, do you want to coach your child because you feel you can best help your child accomplish his or her own dreams, or are you coaching your child to accomplish your own dreams?
- If you coach your own child, will your child come first?

Think carefully. You must be willing to accept your child as he or she is, no matter what the ability level or reasons for participating.

Summary

1. Parents influence the decisions about their children's participation in sport.
2. A coach–parents meeting is a useful way to communicate your expectations to parents. The meeting should be carefully planned.
3. Coaches can have an influence on parents' behaviours on the sidelines.
4. An effective working relationship (coach–parents) is enhanced by keeping the channels of communication open.
5. Some parents pressure their children through guilt when children do not meet their parents' expectations.
6. Some parents tend to increase pressure on their children by expressing their sacrifices, both financial and time.
7. Some parents believe that pressure is good for their children and force their children to work beyond their capabilities or desires.
8. Some parents create pressure when they expect their children to follow in the footsteps of other family members who were great sport achievers.
9. Most parents are encouraging and supportive of their children's participation in sport.
10. Parents should not coach their own children.

Further Reading

American Sport Education Program (1994), *SportParent,* Champaign, IL: Human Kinetics.
Anshel, M. (1990), *Sport Psychology: From Theory to Practice,* Scottsdale, AZ: Gorsuch Scarisbrick.
Loehr, J. and Kahn, E.J. (1989), *Parent-player Tennis Training Program,* USA: Stephen Greene.
Martens, R. (1989), *Successful Coaching,* Champaign, IL: Human Kinetics.
Rotella, R.J. and Bunker, L.K. (1987), *Parenting your Superstar: How to Help your Child get the Most Out of Sports,* Champaign, IL: Leisure.
Thompson, J. (1995), *Positive Coaching,* Portola Valley, CA: Warde.
Williams, J.M. (1993), *Applied Sport Psychology: Personal Growth to Peak Performance,* Mountain View, CA: Mayfield.

Chapter 11

The Balancing Act

- Time Management
- Facility and Equipment Management

If the only responsibility we had in our lives was coaching, we would probably all cope fairly easily. Similarly, coaching would be less stressful if we always had access to the specific facilities and equipment we needed when we wanted them. In this chapter we recognise that most, if not all, coaches have many demands placed on them at once and that venues and equipment are often shared with other teams, sports or activities. Because coaches have a limited amount of time, they have to learn to balance the demands of family, schools, clubs, jobs, professional organisations and friends.

SO MUCH TO DO AND SO LITTLE TIME.

Time Management

- Have you ever put off something important until later?
- Do you have trouble saying 'NO' when people ask you to do things for them?
- Do you do your best work under pressure?
- Do you ever start new projects before finishing current projects?
- Do you find that you rarely have time to do the things you want to do?

If you answered 'yes' to one or more of these questions, you may have some trouble managing your time. The perception (whether actually true or not) that you do not have enough time to do everything you should, is one of the most common sources of stress. When we do not accomplish everything we think we should, we often feel compromised, frustrated and stressed.

A useful way to start evaluating your management of time is to first discover how you currently spend your time. There are 168 hours in every week. Very few people are able to make the most of this time on a regular basis.

ACTIVITY

Consider how you spend your time during an average week. In Weekly Timetable 1 (on the following page), fill in your committed time. Be sure to include some sleep time as committed time. To be completely accurate with this task, actually record how you spend your time during one week. Be sure to pick a week that is fairly representative of your typical lifestyle. (Remember to use pencil or photocopy activities.)

When you have finished the first timetable, calculate how many hours of flexible or free time you have. Do you have time for relaxation? Is your life balanced? Circle the activities which cause you the most stress.

Now that you have some idea how you use your 168 hours each week, begin with a blank timetable (Weekly Timetable 2 is provided) and block in the activities that you feel absolutely must be done every week. Once again, be sure to include time for sleeping. Once the committed time has been scheduled, then allocate time for recreational activities and relaxation. If possible, try to have at least a bit of relaxation time either before or after the activities that cause you the most stress. To some extent we are all restricted in the structure of timetables by work, family, training times and the like. The idea, however, is to try and create a timetable that allows for a balanced lifestyle. Try to adhere to this new schedule and determine if it is realistic.

SELF-REFLECTION

After trialing your new schedule for a week, answer the following questions.

- How easy or difficult was it to stick to your new schedule?
- Were you better able to cope with stressful activities during the week?
- Is there anything you accidentally left out of your schedule that should be included?

Weekly Timetable 1

Hours	Mon	Tues	Wed	Thurs	Fri	Sat	Sun
4–5AM							
5–6							
6–7							
7–8							
8–9							
9–10							
10–11							
11–12							
12–1							
1–2PM							
2–3							
3–4							
4–5							
5–6							
6–7							
7–8							
8–9							
9–10							
10–11							
11–12							
12–1							
1–2AM							
2–3							
3–4							

Weekly Timetable 2

Hours	Mon	Tues	Wed	Thurs	Fri	Sat	Sun
4–5AM							
5–6							
6–7							
7–8							
8–9							
9–10							
10–11							
11–12							
12–1							
1–2PM							
2–3							
3–4							
4–5							
5–6							
6–7							
7–8							
8–9							
9–10							
10–11							
11–12							
12–1							
1–2AM							
2–3							
3–4							

- Was your relaxation time well placed?
- What changes do you think you should make to your schedule?
- Do you need to negotiate with others to make your schedule more balanced?
- Do you think you wasted much time during the week?

Time-wasting

All of us are capable of wasting time. We might waste time by watching TV, listening to music, talking on the phone, raiding the refrigerator, reading novels and magazines, taking naps, shopping, or having long baths or showers. These activities are not bad activities in themselves. But, when coaches are feeling stressed because they have not accomplished everything they wanted and at the same time have spent hours doing some of the above, they should consider how their time is wasted. Scheduling relaxation time is not wasting time, however participating in relaxing activities when we should be doing other things could be considered as wasting time.

ACTIVITY

List the three most common ways you waste time (Meetings at work cannot be included in this list!) Do not include activities that are commitments you have with your job or your family.

1.

2.

3.

POINT TO PONDER
What strategies might you use to overcome these time-wasters?

Procrastination

Procrastination is another way we manage to waste time. Procrastinating and putting things off, however, are not exactly the same thing. What distinguishes the two is the level of discomfort created. Procrastinating has a negative effect. If Carol procrastinates about watering her plants, they die (a definite negative effect). Similarly, if Kent procrastinates about cleaning the house, although no permanent negative consequences may result, there is still the negative effect of feeling guilty. The same activity (or rather non-activity) could be just putting something off for one person and procrastinating for another. Take, for example, the task of cleaning your windows at home. If you do not mind having dirty windows and the people you live with do not mind having dirty windows, failing to clean the windows is not an act of procrastination. If, however, you feel guilty when you have dirty windows or someone else criticises you for not cleaning the windows, then failing to clean them is an act of procrastination. Similarly, whether or not waiting to repair or replace specific sporting equipment is an act of procrastination is dependent on the potential negative effects of waiting. If there are feelings of guilt or harassment, or someone gets injured using the old equipment, then it is procrastination.

One way to counteract procrastination is to set goals. Chapter 5 discussed the goal-setting process. This process can be used to help manage time, prevent stress and complete those tasks that seem to hang over your head.

ACTIVITY

Think of an activity about which you procrastinate. Think of something that really bothers you because you have not done it. Some examples are completing a home project, getting your car serviced, making a dental appointment, getting a haircut, writing letters, paying or getting insurance, taking a holiday, playing with the kids, having coffee with friends, cleaning the bathroom or mowing the lawn.

Now, set a short-term, realistic, positive, controllable and specific goal (see Chapter 5) regarding something you will do in the next week about the activity about which you procrastinate. Specify exactly when you will do it. If necessary, determine a number of strategies that could be used to help you achieve the goal.

Source of procrastination: ....

Short-term goal: ....

....

When will this be achieved? ....

Strategies: ....

....

....

....

Making Lists

Another useful technique to enhance your time management is to create a 'To Do' list. Some people feel they have so many things to do that they do not know where to start. Instead of sitting around feeling overwhelmed, it can be beneficial to create a 'To Do' list and then establish priorities. Be careful with this technique, however, as some people take it to the extreme and end up wasting time by writing and rewriting lists. Used properly though, this technique allows you to become more decisive about time, overcome procrastination and determine your priorities.

ACTIVITY

1. Write a personal 'To Do' list. Write for 2–3 minutes without censoring what you are writing.
2. Establish priorities for your list using A's, B's and C's. (A = absolutely, positively must do; B = really should do; C = would be nice to do).
3. Prioritise the A's using A1, A2, A3 ... (you can only have one A1).
4. On a fresh piece of paper write the A1 activity at the top, then write down all the activities you should do to achieve your A1 activity.
5. Go through the new list and prioritise them with A's, B's and C's.
6. Prioritise your new A's using A1, A2 ...
7. DO WHATEVER YOUR NEW A1 ACTIVITY IS.

You may have noticed that very little mention has been made of coaching so far in this chapter. Learning to manage your time better, however, can make you a less stressed coach. You will be less prone to stress-related illnesses, more relaxed and probably a lot happier overall if you are not stressed about how you are going to get everything done. You will also probably be a more patient and understanding coach.

Keep in mind that the time-management approaches mentioned in this chapter may also be useful for athletes. Very few athletes only train for their sport. Most also have commitments with school, university, friends, family and/or jobs. After completing the activities in this chapter, you should be able to help the athletes with the same process.

Facility and Equipment Management

Because of the multiple demands placed upon coaches, they need to balance their time. Similarly, venues (and equipment) are in demand by many groups and activities and therefore need to be managed in a manner that allows balanced access. There is nothing worse than arriving at a sporting event and finding out that the secretary of the club has no key to the sporting shed and there is no way of getting the goals out for Saturday morning competitions. So, what do you do? Panic? Send all the athletes and parents home? Or improvise? How many times have you been forced to improvise – hundreds? Well what could you have done to prevent this from happening? Has it happened since?

This section is about facility and equipment organisation and safety. Most coaches have an association with a sporting organisation. It is extremely important at the beginning of the season to organise training times and facilities. Approach your sport's organisation for equipment and facility bookings before the season starts. There have been many coaches who meet their team for the first time in the season and do not have enough equipment for all. Many times, coaches have a difficult time in ensuring that athletes are on-task at training without the required equipment (see Chapter 4).

180   The Coaching Process

'WHO BOOKED THE GYM?'

ACTIVITY

You are just meeting your team/squad for the first time. List all the equipment you will need to coach for the year. Remember to include minor equipment such as witches' hats, bibs, stop watches and anything else you need to organise drills or ensure your athletes are safe. An example follows:

Equipment/Facilities to be Booked	With Whom do I need to Book the Equipment/Facility	–	Contact Number
Soccer Field @ 4 p.m., Wed.	R.U. Watching, Maintenance	–	555 1234
Soccer goals	Secretary, Joan Mackie	–	555 1111
Soccer balls (11)	Secretary, Joan Mackie	–	555 1111
Bibs	Happiness School	–	555 1212
Witches Hats (12)	Happiness School	–	555 1212
Uniforms	Secretary, Joan Mackie	–	555 1111
Goalie gloves	Secretary, Joan Mackie	–	555 1111
Mouthguards, shin pads, soccer boots	Athletes are to arrange to get these		

Your turn:

Equipment/Facilities to be Booked	With Whom do I need to Book the Equipment/Facility — Contact Number

Sometimes the sporting organisation you are associated with is not as well planned as you are. You will have to be proactive and take the first step to contact the people who can help you provide a safe and effective learning environment. It would be useful to attend your sport's organisational meetings and learn the way the organisation is managed and run. Promote your sporting organisation. There are too many coaches and parents who complain and are reactive to any initiatives put forward. For the betterment of your team, be proactive and participate in the club decisions. By being proactive, you will be able to seek the best ways to provide effective training sessions for the athletes.

Safety First

Recently there has been a growing concern about liability and negligence in coaching. Coaches have a responsibility to ensure they provide reasonable care and protection of the athletes against predictable risks inherent in the sport. If coaches fail to provide such care, they are considered to be negligent. If a coach is allegedly negligent, they owe some type of duty to a person who may be injured. If coaches have been negligent in their duty, then they are liable to the person who is injured. It is important for coaches to consider the implications of their responsibility or duty of care for the athletes. As part of that duty, they should ensure the equipment and facilities are safe for use.

ACTIVITY

For each of the following cases, decide who is responsible for the actions:

Case Study One

You are coaching softball with a group of 12-year-olds for a local club. You would like to work on batting, so you have brought out all the bats to begin practising. You have asked the children to leave the bats where they are and you turn to go and get the rest of the equipment. When your back is turned, one of your players picks up a bat and begins swinging it around. When swinging, a piece of the bat goes flying and hits another child in the head. The other child is rushed to the hospital with a suspected skull fracture. Who is responsible? What are the implications for you as a coach?

Case Study Two

You are coaching a senior team (A Grade) during a soccer game. It has been raining for three days and the grounds are quite wet. You arrive at the game and notice huge mud puddles and a hole in the middle of the field. When the referee arrives, you ask her to have a good look at the field as you have noticed a big hole in the middle. The referee surveys the field and declares the field safe. Just before half time, one of the players from the other team steps in the hole and breaks her leg and is rushed to the hospital. Who is responsible for the player's injury? What are the implications of this accident for you as a coach?

Case Study Three

You are coaching a group of children in yachting. When you are out in the middle of the harbour, one of the P class boats breaks in half and sinks quickly to the bottom. As Matthew abandons the yacht, he hits his arm on the mast. His arm is broken and as you pick him out of the water you notice the injury. This is the first time that you did not check the boats before putting them in the water, but the club president indicated that he had checked all the boats. You assumed that he checked all the boats thoroughly and had no reason to question his judgement. Who is responsible for Matthew's injury? What are the implications for you as a coach?

It is the coach's responsibility to provide athletes with as safe a facility as possible with well-maintained equipment and in proper condition for use. Coaches are responsible for eliminating unsafe equipment and facilities. It is also their responsibility to inform the club or the facility manager when facilities and equipment are in need of repair or are inadequate. Coaches cannot ensure absolute safety (although they must take every step to do so), but they must provide and maintain facilities relatively free from injury-producing conditions. Coaches are primarily responsible for the area in which the athletes are participating (the coaching area), in fact most of the responsibility for keeping that area safe is the coach's. The sport area should be inspected regularly and warnings given to athletes of potential hazards. Coaches should recommend changes required to unsafe areas, to the sporting organisation. If there is nothing done about a hazard that is noticed, coaches are responsible for protecting the area or piece of equipment. They can do this by not allowing athletes to use the facility or equipment, or by insisting on the use of protective gear to ensure safety.

Facilities

Facilities that are poorly maintained, improperly designed, contain defective equipment, and are eroded by weather pose risk to athletes. Some common injury causes are holes in the field, broken bottles on the facility (not uncommon where facilities have clubhouses attached), sharp objects that stick out into a participation area or equipment that is not a permanent fixture. Some facilities are improperly designed. There are some gyms where the walls are too close to the participation area or bars and other hanging equipment are in the way. If you notice defects, let the sporting organisation know and have the equipment removed or put up protective devices to reduce the risk of injury. As a coach, you have a partial responsibility for requesting upgrading or new facilities. You should be aware of various funding schemes for which your club/school or team may be eligible to upgrade facilities and enhance safety.

Defective equipment in facilities is a common cause of injury. Basketball hoops can be improperly designed for dunking or soccer goals may not be permanent fixtures and can collapse. Defective equipment should be recorded and reported to the proper authorities. If the equipment is defective, do not allow athletes to use it.

Sometimes, the weather can play havoc with facilities. Rain may create deep mud and holes in fields or wet gym floors through leaky roofs. Athletes should not be allowed to use faulty facilities. Coaches should do as much as possible to reduce the risk, although it is impossible to entirely eliminate safety hazards.

To ensure the facility is safe, there are some guidelines you can follow.

- Ensure that proper standards are applied. Ensure athletes do not use a facility that has been declared unsafe and warn athletes about using such an unsafe facility.
- Conduct regular inspections to ensure the facility is safe and properly maintained for the sport.
- Make facility rules and enforce them. Educate athletes about procedures in case of emergencies.
- Ensure there are preventive maintenance strategies for the facility. To follow up on an inspection, ensure the unsafe conditions are fixed and then maintained.
- Share the responsibility amongst members from the sporting organisation including other athletes, coaches, parents and administrators.

Equipment

Equipment supplied by sporting organisations needs to be thoroughly checked to ensure safety. Some sporting organisations provide protective gear. As there are different sizes of athletes, some gear may not fit properly. Coaches should ensure that the athletes receive gear that fits and will protect them. A recent example of questionable equipment is the use of bicycle helmets. There has been much research into how the helmets should be worn and how helmets should fit various sizes of heads. Yet, there have been quite a few instances of bicycle accidents, where if the helmet had fitted well and had been worn properly, head injuries could have been prevented.

Much of what applies to ensuring facility safety can be said about equipment. Some considerations are the proper use of equipment, appropriate equipment selection, the provisions of warnings to players about hazards and knowledge about current equipment safety issues.

Athletes are notorious for trying out unusual ways to use sports equipment. Coaches must ensure that equipment is used correctly and monitor the athletes' use of equipment in a safe facility. When selecting equipment to buy, be sure that current standards of safety are met for each piece.

Coaches are also responsible for instructing athletes in the proper use of equipment. Many pieces of equipment carry a warning message. Athletes should be aware of such warnings. It is also important for coaches to set standards for the use of equipment. For example, if there is a mini-tramp in the gym you use, warn against its use without supervision or permission. Protective equipment is essential to many of our sports, and it is the coach's responsibility to ensure the proper protective equipment is worn. For example, if participation in the sport involves body contact, then athletes should wear mouthguards and possibly headgear.

Some general guidelines for coaches to think about in ensuring a safe environment include:

- Take reasonable safeguards to notice and fix any hazard. Ensure that general conditions of a sporting activity involve no unnecessary risks (such as playing with broken equipment)
- Appropriately limit the number of participants using equipment and a facility at any one time.
- Give instructions and warnings about existing or potential risks.
- Be sure to have efficient and thorough monitoring to protect all athletes.
- Use reasonable care in selecting and fitting equipment, including protective gear.
- Remove obstacles from the participation area. Ensure equipment is arranged for safe participation.
- Conduct regular safety inspections of equipment and facilities.
- Record and report any unsafe equipment or facilities.

Coaches have a responsibility to organise the use of facilities and equipment as well as ensuring the safe use and maintenance of facilities and equipment for athletes. It is impossible to design a completely safe facility and probably impossible to develop completely safe equipment. However, it is up to coaches to take every possible safeguard to provide a safe environment for athletes.

ACTIVITY

List all the sporting equipment and facilities you need to conduct your sport. Be sure to include protective gear and the types of facilities you need to run an effective sport training session. In the last column, list some common maintenance concerns and possible concerns about the facilities (an example follows).

Rock Climbing and Abseiling	Common Concerns, Risks	Safety Precautions, How to Care for Equipment to Ensure Safety
Equipment		
Rope	Fraying, pressure,	Supervise knots, keep a usage log, check ropes before use, include karabiners for connections
Harnesses	Rips, fit on participant, if tested before using	Keep a usage log, ensure the harness fits the climber, tie-in separate from abseil harness
Belay devices	Broken	Supervise tie-ins and belays, test before using
Descendeurs	Broken	Test before using
Anchors	Broken	Establish backups, separate anchors for protection
Protective Gear		
Mats	Mats not in place, not thick enough, holes or worn areas	Ensure mats are in place and that they are fully maintained, with no holes or wearing
Helmets	Cracks, don't fit well	Examine helmets for use, ensure warning signs are placed in a helmet and adhered to by participants
Shoes	Worn rubber, don't fit well	Ensure shoes can grip, not too worn
Facilities		
Rock wall	Loose footsteps, mats not in place, climbers alone	Ensure no loose rocks and that footsteps are secure, put mats in place to protect from fall, no solo climbing
Cliff face		
Spectating area	Spectators get hit by falling rocks	Clearly designated area for spectators with no hazard of being in the line of falling rocks

Now it is your turn to list your safety concerns.

Your Sport	Common Concerns, Risks	Safety Precautions, How to Care for Equipment to Ensure Safety
Equipment		
Protective Gear		
Facilities		

Summary

1. There are 168 hours every week and time management enables coaches (and athletes) to make the most of this time.
2. Coaches will need to balance the demands of family, schools, clubs, jobs, professional organisations and friends.
3. Allocate time in your busy schedule for recreational activities and relaxation. Relaxation before stressful activities is beneficial.
4. All of us are capable of wasting time.
5. Procrastination is counterproductive and contributes to stress. One way to counteract procrastination is to set goals.
6. Making 'To Do' lists and establishing priorities can enhance time management.
7. Communicate with the local sporting organisation early in the season to book facilities and equipment.
8. As a coach, it is your responsibility to provide reasonable care and protection of athletes against predictable risks in your sport.
9. Negligence is failure to provide reasonable care.
10. Common facility risks include poor maintenance, improper design, defective equipment and weather erosion.
11. Common risks relating to equipment include lack of protective equipment, improperly fitted equipment, poorly maintained equipment, lack of appropriate coach supervision, and failure to adhere to warnings about equipment use.

Further Reading

Fewell, M. (1995), *Sports Law: A Practical Guide,* Sydney, Australia: Law Book Company.
Kozoll, C.E. (1985), *Coaches' Guide to Time Management,* Champaign, IL: Human Kinetics.
Nygaard, G. and Boone, T.H. (1985), *Coaches' Guide to Sport Law,* Champaign, IL: Human Kinetics.

Section V

Continuing to Develop as a Coach

Chapter 12

What Now?

- Self-reflective Analysis
- Continuing to Develop as a Coach
- Sharing Ideas

In the discussion of the coaching process thus far, we have seen that effective coaching involves a complex web of decisions and strategies which surrounds a core function of instructing athletes in tactics, skills, daily responsibilities and fundamentals of the sport. We have defined an effective coach as one who allows for maximum individual development within a particular sport. This last chapter reviews the concept of self-reflective analysis and introduces coaches to a self-directed training approach to enhance coaching effectiveness.

A self-directed training approach involves the application of information that has been gained and practised, including self-reflective analysis, using this book. The aims of the approach include:

1. To develop an understanding of coaching strategies used in various coaching environments.
2. To develop the ability to *self-reflect*. This approach will facilitate the evaluation of the effectiveness of instructional strategies (coaching behaviours) in coaching.
3. To develop a self-directed instructional package to facilitate desired changes in coaching strategies.
4. To develop the ability to provide players/athletes with a quality learning experience.

Self-reflective Analysis

In any sport, if athletes cannot perform basic physical and mental skills or understand fundamentals of the sport, it is difficult for them to be able to achieve a high standard of performance. This applies to the coaching process. If coaches do not have the basic skills or understand the fundamentals of coaching, it is difficult for them to achieve a high standard of coaching performance. As part of coach education, it is your responsibility to practise effective coaching strategies. A successful, effective coach should practise and understand the theoretical elements of sport as well as the fundamentals of instruction. This book has provided you with some guidelines for instructional and psychological strategies in coaching. We have given you opportunities to practically apply some strategies through a coaching process labelled self-reflection. Self-reflection is a tool that empowers coaches to continue analysing their coaching.

By continuing to view videotapes of themselves coaching, coaches can perform a subjective self-reflective analysis using their knowledge about coaching. To supplement self-reflective analysis, we provide a list (not comprehensive) of coaching behaviours for self-reflection exercises. Such exercises will help coaches identify and analyse certain behaviours in their own coaching.

SELF-REFLECTIVE ANALYSIS.

A Summary of Coaching Behaviours

Included in this section is a list of coaching behaviours that coaches may notice when observing and analysing their own or their colleagues' work. They are behaviours to do with the coaching strategies of organising, managing, instructing and communicating. Definitions and examples of the behaviour are given. The main coaching action is in bold type. Use the definitions as a resource to help you when using a self-directed training approach (discussed later). Also use this list to identify coaching behaviours you are satisfied with and wish to keep or any for which you would like to design a plan of action to improve or any you wish to eliminate. Although this list is not complete, it gives an indication of behaviours you may wish to consider.

Informative Feedback (see Chapter 7) – **The coach provides information which conveys to the athlete that her or his performance *was* satisfactory or is *becoming* satisfactory and that he or she can continue.** The information indicates one of two things, (1) the performance was satisfactory and should be repeated in the same manner; or (2) the performance was satisfactory but can be improved even further by incorporating additional features. Informative feedback can concern both skill and general behaviours and *must* stipulate what to do on the next occurrence of behaviour. Examples are: 'The entry into the water was fine, but if you point your toes, it will be smoother'; 'The release of the bowl was adequate, if you bring your arm back a bit further, you will get more power'.

Positive Feedback (see Chapters 5 and 7) – **The coach openly demonstrates pleasure with the behaviour of an athlete, group or team.** The feedback is given in a rewarding way and can be verbal or nonverbal. This behaviour is different from informative feedback in two ways: (1) it is purely directed at a past performance; and (2) it carries no instruction for future athlete behaviour. Examples are: 'Great to see that Brooke is first in line'; and, 'It was superb that you held your position for five seconds'.

Cues (see Chapters 4 and 7) – **The coach provides verbal or nonverbal cues to remind the athlete of previous information about performance.** The 'cues' behaviour is different from informative and positive feedback in that the skill has *not* already been performed and the coach wants the athlete to recall specific information already given, for the next performance. Examples are: 'Fingers spread'; 'Remember to put your right foot first'.

Hustle – **This refers to the verbal comments by the coach intended to motivate the athlete to intensify her or his performance** such as 'hurry', 'faster', 'come on'.

Correcting Feedback (see Chapter 6) – **The coach provides information which conveys to the athlete that her or his performance *was not* satisfactory and how it must be altered to continue.** The content should include the performance characteristics that must be introduced to produce at least a satisfactory performance. This contrasts with informative feedback in that (1) the athlete has not yet achieved an adequate performance, and (2) the coach *must* stipulate what to do on the next occurrence of the behaviour. Examples are, 'You should be doing left-hand lay-ups on the left side'; and 'The racquet is too high in your back swing, lower it'.

'Don't' Feedback (see Chapters 3 and 6) – **The coach openly displays displeasure with the skill as it is performed by an athlete group, or team.** 'Don't' feedback conveys negative feelings about, or unacceptability of, the skill or skills performed. It can be verbal or nonverbal. 'Don't' feedback is different from correcting in that the informational content does not indicate what to do on the next occurrence. Examples are: 'Don't drop the ball!'; 'Don't fall in!'.

Witticism (see Chapter 2) – **A remark made by the coach often involving sarcasm, irony or ridicule.** The remark has an element of jest. Examples are: 'You throw like a girl'; 'You are such a wimp'.

High-order Questioning (see Chapter 6) – **The coach asks a question related to the subject matter.** The subject matter is the focus of the session or moment. A high-order question, can elicit a multitude of answers. Examples are: 'Why do you want to get away from your defence?'; 'What is the best way to get to a free space?'.

Low-order Questioning (see Chapter 6) – **The coach asks a question related to the subject matter. There is only one correct answer.** Examples are: 'What side do you throw from?'; 'What colour is the ball?'

Demonstrating (see Chapter 6) – **The coach provides a physical or visual demonstration of a skill or principle of a skill to the team.** The demonstration can be given by either the coach or an athlete.

Directing (see Chapter 4) – **The coach directs an athlete, group or team to do something.** The content does not refer to previous behaviour. Examples are: 'Come in everyone'; 'Get into groups of three'.

Explaining (see Chapter 6) – **The coach clarifies, elaborates or summarises material or paraphrases a statement that was not understood previously.** The content must be related to the subject matter. This will occur commonly when new information is being presented. An example is when the coach is providing the information about how to do the next drill.

Justifying (see Chapter 6) – **The coach rationalises through explanatory remarks, direction, or information given to the athlete.** An example is after the coach has provided information about the paddle stroke and follows up with 'We use this to get more momentum to go forward'.

Organising (see Chapter 4) – **The coach engages in behaviours that lead up to, but are not directly related to, a learning situation or the subject matter.** An example is when a coach passes out bibs or organises the starting line-up for the next competition.

Transition (see Chapter 4) – **A transition is the time it takes to move from one drill to another, or the coach changes the focus, the team changes courts, or similar situations occur that involve changing from one task to another or from one variation of a task to another.** An example in athletics is when athletes have finished the high leg lifts and are moving onto sprint work.

Observing (see Chapter 7) – **The coach is observing athletes and their execution of a skill or performance.** Examples are where there is a break from coach talk and the coach appears to be analysing an executed skill of an athlete or when the coach is observing the way in which a team is executing game strategies.

Socialising – **The coach is communicating to athletes on a topic not related to the subject matter.** An example is when the coach is talking to an athlete about her or his friend, or about what the athlete did on the weekend.

Listening (see Chapter 5) – **The coach displays signs of trying to understand what an athlete is saying.** Signs include eye contact with the athlete(s), silence, or nodding of the head.

ROLLing (see Chapter 5) – **This is a communication behaviour that focuses on the use of nonverbal language. ROLLing is when a coach is talking one on one with an athlete.** The coach remains relatively *Relaxed* with the athlete during the interaction, the coach faces the athlete and adopts an *Open* posture, the coach *Leans* towards the athlete at times and the coach *Looks* at the athlete when communicating with him or her.

Coaches can apply self-reflective analysis to their own experience using these definitions of behaviours. The process of self-reflection involves the skills of observation, analysis, modification and re-evaluation of coaching behaviours which you have been developing in working through this book.

ACTIVITY

Look at a videotape of any coaching session for 15 minutes. Using the list of coaching behaviours from above, identify two behaviours that you think the coach should change. By practising this activity, you will be able to develop your observation and analysis skills and be able to help other coaches in their self-reflection.

Modifying one's own skills requires competence in applying the results of one's observations and analyses. Coaches can learn to modify their skills by applying instructional and psychological theory (some of which is in this book) to their coaching processes. You have participated in this modification process already, but should continue the process to further develop as a coach. Examples of questions that will develop modifying skills include, 'What is it about the behaviour that I need to change?', or 'How will I go about making the change?'

The next step – re-evaluating yourself – requires the same competence and understanding of instructional and psychological theory and involves asking questions like 'How did the change go?', 'Was the change effective for me and the athletes?', or 'What more (if anything) could I do to improve?'.

In summary, the coaching process involves five steps: (1) Observing and collecting information about your coaching; (2) Analysing your collected information based on your and others' knowledge; (3) Using the information to create a plan to change coaching behaviours; (4) Executing the plan (plan of action); and (5) Evaluating the plan of action.

Self-reflective analysis in coach education is based on constant evaluation and modification. Reflective questions should be included as part of an ongoing self-analysis. Reflective questions provide structured guidelines and information about coaching behaviours. Some reflective questions are provided in this book, but coaches should seek sport-specific personnel or other respected individuals and ask them to help develop reflective questions about a particular strategy that they would like to analyse or change. This expert or respected individual would also be a good source for advice about your coaching. Refer to self-reflection activities in Chapters 4, 5, 6 and 7 to help formulate these questions.

ACTIVITY

Write reflective questions for two coaching behaviours you identified in the last activity. You can use this book, other readings that have been suggested in this book, your own intuition based on the behaviour or ideas from other colleagues. You may have to do some research, but once you formulate such questions, you will have them to share with other coaches and for your own future use.

Feedback from respected individuals, from either sport specific experts or other coach educators, is useful for coaches in the self-reflective analysis process. The function of the person that provides this feedback is to assist in enhancing and maintaining coaching behaviours. You can obtain feedback by supplying someone with a copy of your videotape. This 'someone' should be a person you respect, someone in your sport, a colleague or another coach. The feedback provided will serve to further identify the behaviours for development and those that are effective. You should also be your own critic and source of feedback, but remember to look for positive coaching behaviours as well. As you improve, 'pat yourself on the back'.

Continuing to Develop as a Coach

Now that you have worked through this book, continue to strive for greater effectiveness on your own. An advantage of using self-reflective analysis in coach education is the ease of application. Once coaches are trained in self-reflection, they can participate in a self-directed training approach when it is suitable to their own needs and time. A self-directed training approach provides coaches with a means to change coaching behaviours at their own learning pace. A self-directed training approach also encourages coaches to share with other coaches and respected individuals so that they can help analyse videotapes and provide useful feedback.

Modify the approach to suit your needs. There are also other ways to determine if you are effective in applying sport science principles to coaching. For example, if you wanted to determine how you applied the biomechanical principles of force to your sport, you could videotape your coaching to observe and analyse how you interpreted and applied the principles, then design a plan to modify the application of these principles.

An Example of a Self-directed Training Approach

The following is an outline of a successful self-directed training approach, a process to help analyse, change or maintain coaching behaviours:

Step 1: Videotape at least two training sessions and do a self-reflective analysis of your instructional behaviours. Identify one or two coaching behaviours that need attention.

Step 2: After identifying coaching behaviours that need attention, develop a plan of action for changing the identified behaviours. Ask yourself 'How can I design a method to improve this behaviour?' Reflective questions about the targeted behaviours can be obtained from a critical friend, another respected individual, or from written resources (like this book or others that have been suggested for further readings).

Step 3: You will need several training sessions to attempt to improve each of the identified coaching behaviours. The first few training sessions will be used to practise the identified coaching behaviour requiring attention. Videotape a training session when you are ready to do a self-reflective analysis of that identified coaching behaviour. Ensure you have prepared some reflective questions to help in the self-reflective analysis.

Step 4: You will then self-reflectively analyse the videotaped session, give the videotape to a critical friend and gather feedback about the application of the instructional strategy (coaching behaviour) identified.

Step 5: Upon receipt of the feedback from the respected individual, repeat the above process for the second instructional strategy (coaching behaviour).

Step 6: After completion of the self-instructional package, videotape one more session to self-reflectively analyse the changed or unchanged instructional strategies (coaching behaviours).

> **POINT TO REMEMBER**
> You should only focus on changing one coaching behaviour at a time. When you are happy with the change, begin to target another. Just as athletes should focus on one skill at a time, coaches should learn and apply one aspect of coaching at a time.

This self-directed training approach is one method that will help you to continue developing as a coach. Use information gathered from this book and create your own self-directed approach. Remember that there are a multitude of coaching behaviours, so analyse your coaching and decide which particular behaviours you wish to improve.

Self-evaluation (Revisited)

An effective method of identifying the coaching behaviours that coaches want to improve is self-evaluation. In the first chapter of this book you were asked to complete a simple self-evaluation form that had you rate strategies you use as a coach and characteristics about yourself on a 10-point scale. The strategies and characteristics included listening, being prepared, being positive, giving effective feedback, being enthusiastic, keeping your cool, treating athletes equally, providing good learning experiences and varying your tone of voice.

Chapter 8 provided an example of a self-evaluation form for an experienced volleyball team. The challenge now is to create a self-evaluation form for yourself, as a coach. Your self-evaluation form may be in a format similar to the one presented in Chapter 8, or you can create an original format. Whatever format is selected, be sure to include a place to record at least one thing you did really well during the session and at least one specific aspect of the coaching performance that you would like to improve. The content should include a combination of the behaviours listed near the beginning of this chapter, the strategies and characteristics used in the simple form in Chapter 1 and other points from this book that are significant to you. Once you have created your self-evaluation form, make multiple photocopies of it and place them in an easy-access folder or binder.

Sharing Ideas

The most important way for coaches to continue developing is to share ideas with others. Coaches are notorious for keeping coaching secrets to themselves. But the best way to learn about effective and ineffective coaching is to talk with other people, including coaches, parents, administrators, athletes and educators. Coaches have insight into what they have experienced, what has worked, what has not worked. You may have a problem in creating a drill to meet an objective, so go to another coach and ask for her or his advice. You are not admitting defeat, but demonstrating a desire to search for knowledge or new methods. It cannot hurt to ask. The worst that can happen is that someone says 'no'.

Parents have had experience raising and dealing with children. Seek out a parent who has dealt with a particular problem that is being experienced with an athlete. Ask for some solutions or where to go for further advice. Parents are often sources of community information. Some will have contacts or friends who may help.

Administrators have answers too. Many sport administrators have coached before. They have seen a variety of coaches pass through their organisations. They have opinions about good and bad ways to do things. You do not have to agree, but they may spark a new idea.

Athletes may have experienced several different coaches. They may have been exposed to drills or methods that they enjoyed and others they hated. Many athletes would be honoured to be asked about what they know or experiences they have had that they can share. Athletes are important people too and they have opinions and desires. We are there for the athletes, so let them have a say about what to do at training or about what strategies to apply during competitions.

Please do not forget the educators (the teachers, lecturers at universities, coach educators). Although there are coaches who may see educators as being in another world, there are many who are available to help. Historically, there has been a gap between educators and coaches, but many coach educators are willing and eager to close this gap. Coaches should be empowered to enhance their effectiveness, thus the focus in the book on self-reflection. Most educators would like to share, to learn from coaches and for coaches to learn from them. It would be useful to the coaching profession for educators and coaches to work together for the benefit of the athletes. The athletes are the most important consideration and we are all responsible for providing high quality learning experiences. Coaches can make a difference by making the step to approach educators for advice. Educators will not have all the answers, but can sprout some ideas and ways of thinking. It has been an intention of this book to bridge this gap by empowering coaches to gain and apply knowledge at their own pace and in their own way.

SHARE IDEAS WITH OTHER COACHES.

As you have participated in the various activities of self-reflection, you should also be able to offer valuable information to other coaches. Ensure that you serve as a critical friend, one who can provide sound advice and at the same time identify the positive aspects of others' coaching.

One last caution. When seeking advice, ensure you get several opinions before taking action. Reflect on the ideas that have been received and relate them to your situation. Using the skills of self-reflection, adapt the ideas to meet your and your athletes' needs. There is rarely only one way.

Activity

Talk to another coach about a particular physical skill that you have been trying to teach your athletes to understand and master. Ask the coach if he or she has a suggestion as to what drill would best be used to practise this physical skill. After you have discussed the new drill, give the coach a drill that has been extremely successful for you. You do not have to be in the same sport, but it would help if your sports are similar in nature, such as team ball sports, or individual fitness work.

> CONGRATULATIONS, THE FACT THAT YOU HAVE USED THIS BOOK MEANS THAT YOU ARE CONTINUING TO DEVELOP AS A COACH. WE HOPE YOU HAVE GAINED SOME USEFUL IDEAS FROM OUR SHARING.

About the Authors

Lynn Kidman is a lecturer in Sports Coaching for the School of Physical Education at the University of Otago in Dunedin, New Zealand. Lynn has coached athletes of various age groups, from ages 5–75, in the sports of swimming, basketball, volleyball, softball, tennis and soccer. Her PhD was earned in the area of self-reflective analysis for coaches, a basis for this book. Lynn and her family, Bob, Matthew and Simon, live in Dunedin. Lynn enjoys watching her children participating in their sporting and academic pursuits, teaching coaches and coaching.

Stephanie Hanrahan is a senior lecturer in sport and exercise psychology for the Departments of Human Movement Studies and Psychology at the University of Queensland. In addition to teaching swimming and ice skating, she has coached volleyball in three countries – novices and state level players, children and adults, males and females. As a psychologist she has worked with athletes and coaches from a wide variety of sports – from ballet to football and from lawn bowls to skydiving. After 17 years of representative volleyball at the open level, Stephanie currently restricts her sporting involvement to local A-grade volleyball, social tennis and swimming.

Index

Abdominal breathing 142, 148
Achievement motivation 45
Affiliation 46–47
Affirmations 143–144, 151
Analysing
    coaching behaviours 194
    decision-making 194
    developing task analysis 120
    skill technique 119–123, 129–130
Anxiety 45–46, 136, 153, 154
    state 46
    trait 46
Arousal
    controlling 137, 148, 150, 153
    lowering and raising 141–143, 148
    optimal 134–135, 140, 141, 148
    over and under 134–135, 142
Athletes 39–54
    and parents 161
    athlete-centred 30, 46–48
    behaviour 69–72
    body build 39, 54
    characteristics 39–46, 54
    fitness levels 40–41, 54
    individual rights 27
    individual differences 39, 54, 82, 134, 140
    organising into groups 76–77
    personality 44–46, 54, 151
    time management 179
Attention
    attentional styles 44–45, 137
    broad/narrow 44–45
    internal/external 44–45
    focus 44, 150, 157
Audiotaping 9

Behaviour(s)
    athletes 69–72, 153
    coaches 153, 189, 190, 191–193, 195, 196
    fair play 25, 30
    parents 162, 164, 165, 169, 172
    problems 19, 70, 71, 72, 73

Children 24, 32, 50, 127, 161, 165, 167, 168–172, 181–182
Coaching
    approach 39, 40
    behaviours 189, 190, 191–193, 194, 195, 196
    continuing to develop 195–196
    during competitions 149–158
    effective 7, 14–15, 20, 87, 88, 110, 157, 189, 195
    philosophy 21, 30–35, 163
    process 7, 14, 20, 189, 193–194
    sharing ideas 196–198
    successful 14–15, 16, 31, 57
    time management 173–179, 186
Cohesion 49
    see 'Team Cohesion'
Communication 86–91
    CRC instruction 84
    goals 97
    listening 86, 88, 89–90, 100, 106, 193, 197
    mental processes 136
    nonverbal 83, 100
    philosophy 30
    reinforcement 83
    ROLLing 88, 100, 193
    understanding 90–91, 100
    with parents 163, 167–168, 172
Competition 149–158
    administrative functions 157
    and opponents 25–26, 30
    equipment 156
    filling time 157
    food 157
    plan 150, 151–153, 157
    travel arrangements 155–156, 157
Concentration 133–134, 135, 141, 146, 149
Control 137, 140, 148, 157
    arousal 141–143
    emotions 154
    imagery 145–146
CRC instruction 84, 100, 128
Critical friend 16, 195, 198

Cue words
    abdominal breathing 142–143
    arousal 143–144, 148
    coaching cues 63, 75, 78, 105, 107, 109, 126, 127, 191
    concentration 146, 147
    mental plan 151, 152, 157
    task analysis 63–64, 78

Demonstrations 103–106, 110
    a skill 103–104, 106, 117, 192
    checking understanding 105–106, 117
    for feedback 106, 127
    modelling 103, 117
    observing 103
    planning, implementing 103–104, 105, 106
    routines for 104–105
    using videotape 104
    vision 42

Enjoyment
    increasing 92–93
    media 18
    of coaching 16, 20
Environment
    conducive to learning 46–48, 57, 92
    familiar, yet challenging 81, 100
    managing 69–73, 78
    on-task 73–77, 78
    positive 70, 73, 78, 81, 100, 163
    safe 82, 100
    self-determination 81
    supportive 81, 168
Equipment
    goals 97
    maintaining 66, 155, 179–186
    management 173, 179–186
    planning 66, 67, 68, 69, 78, 105, 154, 177–180
    respecting 23
    safety 78, 82, 179–186
Equity Issues 26–28
    individual differences 76, 82, 106
    language 28, 106
    normal vs. abnormal 27
    tips to promote 28
Ethics
    code of 26
    definition of 22
    equal opportunity 26–28
    language 28
    legal and moral duty 26
Explanations 106–110
    and demonstrations 106–108, 110, 117
    as direct coaching 106, 117
    checking understanding 108, 117
    effective explainers 108
    introducing a skill 106

planning 106
routines for 106
Extrinsic
    feedback 124, 126, 130
    reasons for coaching 16, 20

Facility management 179–186
    equipment 179, 183, 186
    maintenance 183, 186
    safety 179, 181, 182, 183, 186
Fair play 22–30, 34
    cheating 22
    dignity 23
    equity 23, 26–28
    guidelines 30
    language 28
    officials 23, 24–25
    opponents 23, 25–26
    rules 23, 24
Feedback 119, 123–130, 191–192
    congruent 127–128, 130
    CRC instruction 84, 100, 128
    demonstration 106
    equal distribution 128
    extrinsic 124, 126, 130
    from others 15, 16, 194
    general vs specific 126–127, 128, 130
    informational 43, 123, 129
    intrinsic 124, 130
    nature 127, 130
    nonverbal 123
    the Query Theory 124–125, 130

Goals
    achieving 94–96, 99
    athletes 94, 166
    coaches 94
    mental skills 137, 141
    philosophy 30
    setting – see 'Goal Setting'
    team 52, 54
    time management 178
Goal setting 94–101
    challenging, but realistic 96, 100
    controllable 95, 100, 135
    intensity 94
    long-term 94, 95, 178
    persistence 94
    recording 100
    short-term 94, 95, 98, 99, 178
    specific 96, 97, 101
    strategies 97, 100, 141
Grid system 65–66

Ice-breaking activities 49–50
Imagery 135–136, 150
    control 135–136, 145–146, 148

instant replay 145–146
psychological warm-up 150
scripts 145–146, 148
vividness 135–135, 148
Instructional objectives 59–63, 78
Integrity 21, 22, 34
Intrinsic
feedback 124, 130
motivation 17–18, 92, 93
reasons for coaching 16–17, 20

Learning
attentional style 44
cognitive phase 106, 117, 120
developmental level 65, 119, 127, 128
environment 57, 71
process 15–16, 20, 102, 102, 110, 112, 115, 117, 119, 123, 124, 135, 195

Media 18, 33, 137
Mental plans 149–153, 157
competition plan 151–153, 157
pre-competition routine 151–153, 157
psychological warm-up 150
Mental skills 97, 131–148, 189
Motivation
achievement 45
competence 93
definition 92
direction 92, 100
goal setting 94, 96, 99, 137
intensity 92, 100
intrinsic 17–18, 92, 93
participant 48
persistence 92, 94, 100
Motives to participate 46–48, 54, 93
affiliation 46–47, 54
desire for sensation 46, 47, 54
mastery 46, 47, 54
self-direction 46, 47, 54
social comparison 46, 48, 54

Negligence 181

Observing
coaching behaviours 194
demonstration 103, 105
observation plan 120–123, 129
positioning 121
safety 120–121
skill technique 119–123, 129, 193

Parents 161–172
behaviours 24, 124, 164, 165
coaching own children 171, 172
coach–parents meeting 163–167, 168, 172
communicating 163, 167–168, 196, 197
competitive stress 161, 167, 169
expectations of 168–171
pressures 168–170, 172
Performance
consistency 131–132, 149
enhancing cohesion 49–54
goals 95, 97
mental skills factors 133–148, 149
process 30
skill technique 95, 97, 119, 124–125, 129, 191
Personality 44–46, 54, 151
Philosophy
authors 31–32, 34
coaching 21, 30–35, 163, 165
fair play 23–24
positive 30
writing your 23–24
Positive approach 82–86, 100, 154
communication 86–91
definition 83
encouragement 83, 100
positive wording 69, 71, 72, 85, 100
realistic expectations 84
reinforcement 76, 86
Positive management 57, 77–78
appropriate behaviour 69–70, 78
definition 69–70, 78
desist 73
inappropriate behaviour 72
managing athletes 57
reinforce and praise 70, 72, 76
Pre-competition routine 150–151, 152, 157
Punishment 86

Query theory 124–125, 130
Questioning
directing, distributing 115
guided discovery 115–116, 117
high order 110–111, 117, 192
low order 110–111, 117, 192
movement response 110, 117
planning 111, 117
probing 114–115
problem-solving 110, 117, 124
rhetorical 111
reinforcement 114

Reflective questions
definition and use 9, 15, 194, 195
ROLLing 88–89, 101, 193
Routines
demonstrating 104–105
explaining 106
gathering 106, 109
pre-competition 149, 150–151, 153
questioning 112
Rules 24, 34, 163

Safety 164, 166, 179, 181–186
Sandwich instruction 84, 128
Self-awareness
    athletes 43, 124
    forms 138–139, 148, 151
    mental skills 137–139
    mental state 137, 139–140
    Query theory 124–125
Self-confidence 19, 96, 135, 136, 138, 140, 143–145, 147, 148, 149, 150
Self-control 22, 153–154, 157
Self-determination 81, 93, 100
Self-directed training approach 7, 189, 191, 195–196
Self-evaluation form 16, 148, 151, 196
Self-talk 136, 143–145, 147, 150
Self-reflection
    definition 7, 8, 190
    learning process 15–16, 20, 194
    self-reflective analysis 15, 189–194, 195, 198
    using video 8, 15, 16, 190, 194, 195
Senses 41–43
    balance 41, 43
    hearing 41, 124
    kinaesthetic awareness 41, 43, 124, 125
    touch 41, 42–43, 124
    vision 41, 42, 124
Session planning 57–69, 78
    designing a plan 59–69
    different ability levels 65, 78
    grid system 65
    instructional objectives 59–63
    preparing to coach 67
    training plan 68, 80
Sharing ideas 26, 195, 196–197
Simulations 147, 148, 149
Social cohesion 49, 54
Spectators 24, 30, 124
Sportsmanship 25
Success 7, 13, 14, 21, 30–31, 74, 92, 94, 95, 100

Task analysis 62–63, 78, 106, 120, 122–123, 129
Task cohesion 49, 54
Team cohesion
    benefits of 49–50
    cliques 53, 54
    development of 49–54
    distinctiveness 52, 54
    establishing team goals 52, 54
    ownership 52
    social 49, 54
    task 49, 54
    team building 137
    travel 155
    trust 50, 54
    turnover of players 53, 54
Time on task 73, 78
    flow 76, 78
    management games 76
    managerial task 73–74, 78
    non-managerial task 73–74, 78
    organising athletes 76–77
    positive reinforcement 75–76
    prompts and hustles 75
    routines 75, 78
Time management 173–179, 186
    balanced lifestyle 174
    goals 178
    mental processes 137
    procrastination 177–178
    stress 174–177
    timetabling 174–177
    time-wasting 177
    'To Do' lists 178–179
Travel 155–158

Values and principles 23–24, 26, 44
    attitudes 44
    coaches 21, 22, 32
    philosophy 30, 32–34
    rules 24
Videotaping
    analysing skill technique 120, 124
    athletes 43, 165
    demonstration 104
    self-confrontation 15, 69
    self-reflection 8, 15, 190, 194, 195

Winning 13, 18, 30–31, 95